LATIN IN OUR LANGUAGE

Cum in Britannia, dic ut Britanni

LATIN IN OUR LANGUAGE

by

Peter Barker

with illustrations by
Jonathan Griffin

Bristol Classical Press

This impression 2003
First published in 1993 by
Bristol Classical Press
an imprint of
Gerald Duckworth & Co. Ltd.
61 Frith Street, London W1D 3JL
Tel: 020 7434 4242
Fax: 020 7434 4420
inquiries@duckworth-publishers.co.uk
www.ducknet.co.uk

A catalogue record for this book is available
from the British Library

ISBN 1 85399 376 X

Printed and bound in Great Britain by
Antony Rowe Ltd, Eastbourne

The cover illustration is based on one of the figures from the
sculptured frieze of the Ara Pacis in Rome. The drawings on p. 32
are based on a slave painted on a 4th century BC South Italian
vase and on a sculptured head of the emperor Hadrian.

CONTENTS

PREFACE

After the successful publication of *The Greek We Speak*, John Betts suggested to me that I should produce a similar *The Latin We Speak*. It was immediately apparent that transliteration from a novel alphabet was no longer a central theme, and that the sheer number of Latin words in English gave almost overwhelming scope and necessitated many choices and restrictions. For detailed information on the derivation of words I am much indebted to the *Oxford Dictionary of English Etymology* (edited by C.T. Onions).

This book is emphatically not a study of English etymology as such; rather it seeks to stimulate an interest in words and their formation through a variety of topics and approaches, with differing levels of difficulty even within the individual exercises. My hope is that there is enough easy encouragement for those students starting out from a more limited base, as well as plenty to challenge the more advanced. Similarly my aim has been to make the book comprehensible, with a teacher's assistance, to those who are not learning Latin but would benefit from an acquaintance with some Latin in order to develop their language awareness and enlarge their working English; at the same time the intention is that students who are learning Latin will be able to reinforce their Latin, as well as their English, vocabulary.

While I have been devising and working on the ideas and material now presented in this book I have been encouraged by the interest and support of colleagues at Oundle School, in the English as well as the Classics department, and by the enthusiasm of pupils who have tested some of the preliminary drafts. In particular I am grateful to my colleague Robin Newman for his patient help and instruction in the word processing skills used in setting up this book on an Apple MacIntosh computer; to Jonathan Griffin who has done most of the illustrations for me; and to my wife Gill for her forbearance during the many hours in which this project has absorbed me and for her unflagging confidence in its eventual fruition.

Oundle
January 1993   P.H.B.

vii

INTRODUCTION

This book aims to help you to explore the countless words which have come into our own language from Latin, the language of the ancient Romans once widely spoken throughout the western lands of their empire. My purpose is not to teach you Latin as such; but I hope that, if you are not studying Latin, you will enjoy the opportunity to find out something about it, and that, if you are, you will find using this book a useful way of consolidating your knowledge.

What then is so special about these Latin based words? Their sheer number and variety make them an indispensable part of the richness of the English language; but they are also of particular importance and disproportionate prominence within the whole field of education. Research in Britain and America has shown the educational advantage for school success associated with a wide vocabulary of Latin based words. An awareness of Latin should also improve your spelling and familiarity with some of the regular 'family' patterns in which new words are adapted from existing ones will extend your own verbal range.

Why then has Latin in particular had such an important influence, even many centuries after the fall of the Roman empire? Initially Latin was just one of several Italic languages within the family of related languages known as Indo-European. (Thus Germanic based *seven* is the same Indo-European word as Latin *septem*, not a derivative.) The political success of the Romans turned their particular dialect into a 'world' language and, after the 'barbarian' invasions and collapse of central control, the common Latin spoken in the different provinces gradually developed into the early forms of such modern languages as French, Italian and Spanish. Even the Anglo-Saxons who invaded England borrowed some Latin words.

Medieval English was enriched with many words, of ultimately Latin origin, which were adopted from French, especially Norman French. While French was developing out of vernacular Latin, the spellings tended to reflect contemporary pronunciation and often came to bear little recognisable resemblance to Latin. Some have since been re-Latinized in their spelling; for instance *perfeccioun* in Chaucer has become *perfection*. New words were also being introduced into early French directly from written Latin and these tend to be more recognisable as such. Very many, however, of the Latin derived words mentioned in this book have been introduced into English from the 15th century onwards, especially during and as a result of the Renaissance. The process has continued into the 19th and 20th centuries with many new scientific terms being coined from Latin roots. There are also a number of pure Latin words and phrases which we continue to use.

Latin is an inflected language: that is such things as time, person and the relationships between words are often indicated by changes in the endings of the words rather than by differing word order or the employment of auxiliary words. This means that what is essentially the same Latin word can exist in several differing spellings, a fact which is particularly important with many verbs, as you will see in the vocabulary where a second form of the stem, which gives rise to English derivatives, has been underlined. You will need to use this main vocabulary as well as the word lists on individual pages; an English dictionary too will be useful. Although you will find it helpful to start with the earliest pages in the book, there is no need to stick rigidly to the order throughout. Nearly all the exercises contain a mixture of easy and really challenging questions. By filling in the answers in the spaces provided you will be doing a great deal to create your own reference book, one which I hope you will continue to find useful and interesting for many years.

PREFIXES

Extra syllables (mostly also used as prepositions) could be added as prefixes in front of Latin verbs in order to give them a more specific meaning. These are frequently seen in English derivatives also. The final consonant of the prefix is often adjusted to suit an initial consonant in the basic stem.

a,ab,abs	from, away	ob	in the (opposite)way (of)
ad	to, towards, against	per	through, thoroughly
con,com	with, together, completely	pr(a)e	before, in front, in advance
de	down,down from, aside	pro(d)	before, forward, for
di(s)	apart, in different directions	re(d)	back, again
e(x)	out of, up out of, fully	sub	under (force often obscured)
in	in, into, on, upon	super	above, over, on top, besides
inter	between, among, in between	trans	across

Portable : something which can be **carried** (*porto* = I carry)

____port : I carry back (information)

____port : I carry out (of a country)

____port : I carry into (a country)

____port : I carry across (from one place to another)

____port : I carry (down) away (from a country)

____port : I carry (myself) with

____port : I (help to) carry (from underneath)

Versatile : able to keep changing or **turning** (*verto* = I turn)

____vert : I turn away

____vert : I turn back (cf. ___verse)

____vert : I turn into a different direction (cf. a traffic ___version)

____vert : I turn thoroughly, overthrow or corrupt

____vert : I turn on itself (upside down)

____vert : I change, assimilating with another thing (e.g. £ → $)

____vert(isement) : designed to turn attention towards a product

____verse : turned crosswise (e.g. an engine)

A **vocation** is a **calling** (*voco* = I call)

    ____voke : I call together

    ____voke : I call out

    ____voke : I call in

    ____voke : I call back

    ____voke : I call forth, incite

A **tractor** is used to **pull** or **drag** things (*traho* = I pull)

    ____tract : I pull out (cf. an ____tract, taken from e.g. a book)

    ____tract : I draw towards myself

    ____tract : I take away (from underneath)

    ____tract : I take back again

    ____tract : I extend by dragging forwards

    ____tract : I draw (eg.attention) into a different direction

    ____tract : I withdraw within myself (cf. a ____tract, when two parties agree together)

    ____tract : I withdraw something from (cf. ____tract as noun or adjective)

A **trajectory**: the path of a missile (*traiectus* = having been **thrown** across)

    ____ject : I throw back

    ____ject : I throw under, reduce to obedience

    ____ject : I throw in (with a syringe)

    ____ject : I throw (myself) out (from a plane)

    ____ject : I throw forward (e.g. an image, a film)

    ____ject : I throw in between (a remark perhaps)

    ____ject : I throw down

    ____ject : I throw in the way

    ____ject : thrown away, miserable

    ____jecture : a throwing together, guess

MORE PREFIXES

-gress :   some sort of movement (*-gredior, -gressus* = I go)

_____gress :   a coming together with others

_____gress :   I go forward, a going forward

_____gress :   I go off in a different direction (a __gression)

_____gress :   a going in (cf. the __gred____ for a cooking recipe)

_____gress :   a going out

_____gress :   I go back

_____gression :   a going across the bounds of the permitted

_____gression :   a going against somebody

Ludicrous : absurd; (earlier) witty, jocular, having the character of a **play**
(*ludicrum* = a stage play; *ludo* = I play)

_____lude :   I play upon, refer indirectly to   (an __lusion)

_____lude :   I play along with (in a secret, fraudulent agreement)

_____lude :   I play down, I cheat into a false opinion

_____lude :   I 'play out of', escape from

_____lude :   introductory action, playing beforehand

_____lude :   a space of time in between the performance

_____lusion :   a deception, false perception 'played on' one

Lapse :   a slip or stumble (*labor, lapsus* = I slip, slide, fall)

_____lapse :   I slip back, a slipping back

_____lapse :   I slip out, pass by

_____lapse :   I fall in together

Merger: two businesses (e.g.) plunged in together (*mergo* = I dip, plunge)

_____merge :   I plunge under (water)

_____merse :   I plunge something into

_____merge :   I come out (situation coming up suddenly = _mergency)

Now try selecting a prefix and seeing how many different suffixes you can add to it. Here are some examples to start you off, with vocabulary at the bottom of the page to help you to complete the words:

dis_____	I spread the seed	dis_____	I stretch apart
dis_____	I place apart	dis_____	I break apart
dis_____	I scatter abroad	dis_____	I twist apart
dis_____	I feel differently	dis_____	I make a distinction

(The prefix **dis-** is also used in English words with a
negative or privative force — e.g. *displeasure, dismember*.)

inter_____	I break in between	inter_____	I spread in between
inter_____	among several peoples	inter_____	gap (between ramparts)

pre_____	I shut out in advance	pre_____	element attached in front
pre_____	I foretell, say before	pre_____	buy/take chance before
pre_____	I stretch (a disguise) before myself		
pre_____	a walking in front, preliminary statement		

trans_____	a pouring across	trans_____	I climb across, surpass
sub_____	a boat under the sea	sub_____	existing under the earth
sub_____	I quell, put under yoke	sub_____	I settle down
super_____	I have oversight of	super_____	I come over/besides
super_____	a thing written on top	super_____	over-flowing

ambulo -are	I walk	rumpo -ere (rupt)	I break
cerno -ere	I perceive, see	scando -ere (-scend)	I climb
claudo -ere (clud/s)	I shut	scribo -ere (script)	I write
dico -ere (dict)	I say	semen -inis n.	seed
discrimen -inis n.	difference	sentio -ire	I feel
emo -ere (empt)	I buy	sido -ere	I settle
figo -ere (fix)	I attach	spargo -ere (spars/spers)	I scatter
fluo -ere	I flow	tendo -ere	I stretch
fundo -ere (fus)	I pour	terra -ae f.	land, earth
iugum -i n.	yoke	torqueo -ere (tort)	I twist
loco -are	I place	vallum -i n.	rampart
marinus adj.	of the sea	venio -ire	I come
natio -ionis f.	tribe, people	video -ere (vis)	I see

WHAT DO YOU MAKE OF IT?

— the suffix -FY

-ify has been added to a variety of bases to make new words (e.g. *codify*, *beautify*); modern coinages are often rather trivial or humorous (e.g. *prettify*, *fishify*). Older words with this ending came through French from Latin or late Latin verbs in *-ficare* meaning to make something, or give it a certain state or quality. The vocabulary opposite will help you to fill in the English verb in *-ify* with the given meaning, and the corresponding noun in *-ification*.

_*magnify*_____	I make big	__*magnification*_
_____	I make adequately copious	_____
_____	I make peace	_____
_____	I make clear	_____
_____	I make good, show as righteous	_____
_____	I assess the amount	_____
_____	I give pleasure to	_____
_____	I build up (esp. moral qualities)	_____
_____	I ascertain the truth of	_____
_____	I make holy	_____
_____	I do to death, humiliate	_____
_____	I make one	_____
_____	I affirm (by a written document)	_____
_____	I make a god of	_____
_____	I change the limit or manner	_____
_____	I form branches, branch out	_____
_____	I make bristle or shake with fear	
_____	I make right, straight	
_____	I make soft	
_____	I bear witness	

Some of the Latin verbs ended in *-facere* rather than *-ficare*, although the influence of the latter form in late Latin, and thus in French, has given us verbs in *-fy* or *-efy*.   The corresponding nouns, however, preserve the Latin ending in *-faction*.

_____ I do enough for somebody   _____

_____ I make rotten   _____

_____ I reduce to a flowing state   _____

_____ I make slow-witted, stunned   _____

aedes	house, building	mors mortis	death
amplus	copious, large enough	pax pacis	peace
certus	sure, certain	putridus	rotten
clarus	bright, clear	quantus	how much
deus	god	ramus	branch
gratus	pleasing	rectus	straight
horror	fearful bristling, shaking	sanctus	holy
iustus	righteous	satis	enough
liquidus	flowing	stupeo	I am stunned, amazed
magnus	big, great	testis	witness
modus	manner	unus	one
mollis	soft	verus	true

— the suffix -ATE

Verbs in *-ate* (generally meaning to do something to something) are based on first conjugation Latin verbs, some of which were themselves developed from simple nouns or adjectives; the latter can still give a useful clue, or extra colour, to the meaning of the English word.   Find the key Latin word, without any prefix, in the vocabulary at the back of this book to give the meanings of the following and then check them in your dictionary:

denigrate _____   elucidate _____

annihilate _____   lubricate _____

ameliorate _____   eradicate _____

exonerate _____   desiccate _____

renovate _____   aggravate _____

reiterate _____   integrate _____

procrastinate _____   negotiate _____

illuminate _____   initiate _____

repudiate _____   mitigate _____

INEPT OR INFORMED?

All the following Latin based words begin with 'in' ('im/il' before 'm', 'p' or 'l',. In some words this is the prepositional prefix suggesting 'in/on/into'; but in others the prefix is negative, the Latin equivalent to 'a-' in Greek words (e.g. *atheist*) and 'un-' in Anglo-Saxon and other words (e.g. *unready, untold*). Fill in the meaning of each word in the appropriate column according to the significance of the prefix. You will find the basic Latin words in the vocabulary at the back of this book. If you are unsure about some of the 'in' words in the list you should look them up in your English dictionary.

Negative Prefix		Prefix = 'in/on/into'
unsuited (aptus)	inept	
	inform	_give shape (forma) or knowledge to_
	innumerable	
	infallible	
	incarcerate	
	incessant	
	imbibe	
	inebriated	
	innovate	
	innocent	
	involve	
	impudent	
	invent	
	insomnia	
	improvise	
	impersonate	
	inarticulate	
	inevitable	
	incriminate	

_____	immortal	_____
_____	incantation	_____
_____	incorporate	_____
_____	incur	_____
_____	immaculate	_____
_____	impeccable	_____
_____	immediate	_____
_____	inaccessible	_____
_____	implicate	_____
_____	immigrant	_____
_____	impious	_____
_____	incision	_____
_____	imperturbable	_____
_____	immense	_____
_____	incarnation	_____
_____	impotent	_____
_____	imminent	_____
_____	incident	_____
_____	implore	_____
_____	impugn	_____
_____	impatient	_____
_____	illicit	_____
_____	invigilate	_____
_____	immunity	_____
_____	injury	_____
_____	indolent	_____

PROVERBS

Here are some Latin proverbs. The English equivalents are given below. Match them together and also write in the literal meaning of the Latin if you can.

Festina lente _____

(lit. = _____)

Dum spiro spero _____

(lit. = _____)

De fumo ad flammam _____

(lit. = _____)

Pares cum paribus congregantur _____

(lit. = _____)

Non omne quod nitet aurum est _____

(lit. = _____)

In duabus sellis sedere _____

(lit. = _____)

Bis dat qui cito dat _____

(lit. = _____)

In silvam ligna ferre _____

(lit. = _____)

Quieta noli movere _____

(lit. = _____)

Rem tetigisti acu _____

(lit. = _____)

A friend in need is a friend indeed
All that glitters is not gold
Birds of a feather flock together
Let sleeping dogs lie
More haste, less speed

Out of the frying pan into the fire
To carry coals to Newcastle
To have a foot in each camp
While there is life there is hope
You have hit the nail on the head

QUOTATIONS AND MOTTOES

Here are some common quotations from Latin writers for you to match with their meanings which are given below.

Mens sana in corpore sano _____

In vino veritas _____

Ars est celare artem _____

Dulce et decorum est pro patria mori _____

Quot homines tot sententiae _____

Carpe diem _____

De mortuis nil nisi bonum _____

Non omnia possumus omnes _____

Quis custodiet ipsos custodes? _____

Varium et mutabile semper femina _____

A woman is always fickle and changeable
A healthy mind in a healthy body
As many opinions as there are people
It is sweet and noble to die for country
Make the most of the present

(Speak) only good of the dead
The skill is to conceal the skill
Truth emerges in drink (truth in wine)
We cannot all do everything
Who will guard the guards themselves?

Many families and organizations still use Latin for their mottoes.
e.g.;   _Per ardua ad astra_ ("By endeavour to the stars"): _____
        E pluribus unum ("Out of more, one"):   _____

Many schools too have Latin mottoes.   Some stress the importance of the school itself: _Floreat Etona_ ("Let Eton flourish"), _Membra sumus corporis magni_ ("We are limbs of a great body").   Others stress the need for effort and work: _Conabor_ ("I shall try"), _Dum tempus habemus laboremus bene_ ("While we have time let us work well").   In one school in Gloucestershire the emphasis on work is combined with a warning: _Aut disce aut discede_ ("Either learn or leave")!   Others seek to remind their members of the ultimate aim of learning, either in general terms — _Altiora peto_ ("I seek higher things"), _Meliora sequamur_ ("Let us follow better things") — or more precisely: _Disce prodesse_ ("Learn to be of service"). Others show a religious link: _Verbum Dei lucerna_ ("God's Word, a light").

Does your school have a Latin motto? If not, you could try to invent one.

_____   =   _____

COMBINATIONS

We have seen how different prepositional prefixes can be combined with the same basic verb stem to give a variety of words. The verb stem itself often occurs in two different forms, one used in Latin for the present tense and the other for the past participle passive (usually known as the supine stem). In English most verbs add -ed to form the past participle passive: *I call,* but *(having been) called.* Others, however, are changed considerably: *I bring,* but *(having been) brought .* This is true of many Latin verbs. e.g.:

moveo	I move	motus	(having been) moved
volvo	I roll	volutus	(having been) rolled
fero	I bear, carry	latus	(having been) carried
mitto	I send	missus	(having been) sent

Now see how you can combine a variety of prefixes and suffixes with each form of the Latin stem to produce an even greater collection of related English words. In each case consider how the literal meaning from the derivation underlies the meaning of the English word.

Prefix	Stem	Suffix	English Derivatives
—	mov	e	*Move, movable, motion, motor, motive*
com	mot	ion	
e		able	
re		or	
pro		ive	
		al	

Prefix	Stem	Suffix	English Derivatives
con	volv	e	
de	volut	ed	
e		ion	
in			
re			

con/l	fer	—	
de	lat	e	
dif		ent	
e		ion	
in		ence	
pr(a)e			
re			
suf			
trans			

Interfere actually comes from *inter + ferio* (I strike) and was originally used of a horse hitting one leg against another.

—	mit(t)	—	
ad	mis(s)	ible	
com		e	
dis		ion	
e		ive	
inter			
per			
pro			
re			
sub			
trans			

Even more words can, of course, be formed by introducing other parts of English verbs or by adding an extra suffix or even by using an extra prefix:

> e.g. verbs — mov**ing,** mov**ed** (participles); **differentiate**
> nouns — mov**ement,** mov**er,** admiss**ibility,** different**ial**
> adjectives — emotion**al,** deferent**ial**
> adverbs — emotion**ally,** emot**ively**
> a second prefix — **read**mit, (negative) **in**admissible.

MORE COMBINATIONS

The vowel 'a' in the stem of a Latin verb regularly became 'i' in the present stem and 'e' in the past participle when a compound verb was formed with a prepositional prefix.   This has been followed in English derivatives.

e.g.   facio (factus)   I make or do   conficio (confectus)   I complete
       capio (captus)   I take   accipio (acceptus)   I receive

—	fic	—	
con	fact	ient	
de	fect	ion	
ef		ive	
in		or	
per		ory	
pre		ionary	
pro			
re			

—	cap	—	
ac (ad)	cip	e	
con	capt	ient	
de	cept	ion	
ex		ive	
in		ure	
inter		or	
per		a/ible	
pre			
re			

N.B.   'Receive', 'receipt' etc. come via French from the same Latin root.

Here are two more sets of combinations for you to try:

teneo (tentus) I hold   pono (positus) I put, place

—	ten	—	
abs	tin	ure	
at (ad)	tent	able	
con	tain	ent	
de		ion	
ob		ance	
per			
re			
sus			

N.B. The stem 'tain' comes to us via French.   Indeed very many words have been mediated from Latin through French into English.   Remembering the French connection what do you make of the word 'maintain'?

—	pon	—	
com	pos	e	
de	posit	ent	
dis		ion	
ex		or	
im		ive	
inter		ure	
op			
pro			
sup			
trans			

YET MORE COMBINATIONS

cedo	I yield, go	cessus	
duco	I lead	ductus	(having been) led
scribo	I write	scriptus	(having been) written
solvo	I loosen	solutus	(having been) loosened
venio	I come	ventus	
video	I see	visus	(having been) seen

—	vid	e	
ad	vis	ion	
di		ent	
pro			
re			

—	solv	e	
ab	solut	ent	
dis		ion	
re			

—	ced	—	
abs	cess	e	
ac	ceas	ion	
con	ceed	ure	
de		ent	
inter			
pre			
pro			
re			
suc			

ad	ven	—	
con	vent	ient	
e		e	
in		ion	
inter			
pre			
sub			

ab	duc	—	
ad	duct	e	
con		ion	
con		or	
de		ive	
in			
pro			
re			

—	scrib	—	
a	script	e	
con		ion	
de		ure	
in		ive	
pre			
pro			
sub			
tran			

NOMENCLATURE

nomen = name   nomino -are = I name

An important Roman official might be accompanied by his *nomenclator* whose job was to know and announce the names of those whom his master met. We use the word nomenclature to mean a set of names.

Many English names have developed from Roman names. A typical Roman man had three names: a first name (praenomen) selected from a limited number of such names, some of which originally indicated position in the family (e.g. *Septimus, Quintus* — English *Quentin*); a family or clan name (e.g. *Terentius, Horatius* — English *Terence, Terry, Horatio, Horace*); and an added name (cognomen) indicating the branch of the family or further distinguishing a man by reference to some characteristic or achievement (e.g. *Naso, Germanicus, Paulus* — English *Paul*). Some names were based on geographical locations: e.g. *(H)Adrian*, a man from the Adriatic; *Laurence*, a man from Laurentum a town near Rome.

Other English names have developed out of other Latin nouns and adjectives, usually suggesting desirable concepts or qualities: e.g. *Victor(ia), Constance, Prudence, Virginia, Serena*. Some of these were themselves being used as names in the Roman empire, e.g. *Priscilla* (= "good-old"). Some words have undergone considerable change: *Emil(e)* and *Amelia* are derived from the same Roman family name (*Aemilius*) and *Tish(a)* originated in *Laetitia* (joyfulness). The etymology of names can be tricky: *Rosemary* is a based on two Latin words although the apparent combination of *Rose* and *Mary* may have helped to popularize it; conversely *Rosamund* probably has a Germanic origin and came to us via the Normans but its popularity was enhanced by being interpreted as *Rosa Mundi* (Rose of the World) or *Rosa Munda* (Pure Rose).

In the 'word search' opposite there are 28 boys' or girls' names (all with Latin origins) reading from left to right and downwards, horizontally, diagonally or vertically. (Choose the longest form of the name that can be found.) When you have identified these, the 28 letters which you have not used will make 4 more names (reading from left to right from the top). The vocabularies at the back of the book will help you to match the names you have found in the 'word search' to these clues and then to fill in the names in the spaces provided.

_____	born (on Christmas Day)	_____	a strong girl
_____	speaks the truth	_____	cheerful
_____	a real star	_____	honey sweet girl
_____	conquering man	_____	a kingly boy
_____	a man from the woods	_____	happiness herself

_____ warrior queen		_____ a dear girl
_____ fond of wild animals?		_____ a little fellow?
_____ this boy has added 'h'		_____ a follower of Mars?
_____ a lordly man		_____ a little warrior
_____ an eager rival		_____ revered emperor?
_____ dew of the sea		_____ a noble lady
_____ named after ___ Caesar?		_____ a blind boy?
_____ she makes you happy		_____ warlike with a 'k'
_____ strong. esp. on the 14th		_____ a girl full of light

P	A	U	L	S	Y	L	V	E	S	T	E	R
C	U	L	E	M	T	C	A	M	I	L	L	A
E	S	M	A	R	C	E	L	F	N	T	P	N
E	T	R	E	G	V	A	L	E	R	I	E	T
R	I	I	N	C	E	C	I	L	L	E	E	H
J	N	P	A	T	R	I	C	I	A	U	X	O
M	U	D	O	M	I	N	I	C	M	M	C	N
E	C	L	L	A	T	A	H	I	L	A	R	Y
L	E	M	I	L	Y	T	R	T	E	R	R	C
I	R	O	S	E	M	A	R	Y	L	T	A	K
N	U	D	I	V	A	L	E	N	T	I	N	E
D	I	A	N	A	V	I	N	C	E	N	T	A
A	C	A	R	A	B	E	A	T	R	I	C	E

These spaces are for the four names formed by the letters which remain in the 'word search' after you have found all the names which fit in above.

_____ bright and famous girl		_____ a stranger
_____ merciful man		_____ a lame girl?

NUMERACY

numerus = number   numero -are = I count

Latin numerals, both cardinal (one, two, three etc.) and ordinal (first, second, third etc.) are much used in English words. Use the information in the table to answer the questions and fill in the blanks below.

I	unus	primus
II	duo	secundus
III	tres,tria	tertius
IV	quattuor	quartus
V	quinque	quintus
VI	sex	sextus
VII	septem	septimus
VIII	octo	octavus
IX	novem	nonus
X	decem	decimus
C	centum	
M	mille (pl. milia)	

singuli = 1 at a time
bini = 2 at a time

quadri- = 4 fold

septuaginta = 70

multi = many
plures = more
universi = all

Why are the last four months of the year so named?   The Roman year originally consisted of only ten months, the first of which was named in honour of _____ , Romulus' father.

_____

Two of the months were originally named **Quintilis** and **Sextilis**.   After whom were they renamed with the names we still use?

_____

A **quinquennial** inspection is carried out every ___ years. _____

plants have a life cycle of two years and a **millenium** is a period of

_____ years.

A **sextet** is a group of ___ musicians.   Five are called a _____ and

four a _____ ;   two can play a _____ , but three are

needed for a _____ .

A car with pedals for both instructor and pupil has _____ controls.

The system of counting in tens is called _____ ;   that of counting in

twos is called _____ .

Unilateral parking confines parked cars to _____ side of the road; _____ talks take place between two sides at a time, whereas many groups are represented in _____ talks and ___ parties can participate in **tripartite** negotiations.

"School **decimated** by 'flu!"   If there are 1,000 pupils, how many have succumbed to the virus? _____

After **primary** and _____ schools some students go on to _____ education.

A **unicorn** has _____ horn; a **centipede**, if the name were to be trusted, would have _____ feet (pedes) and a **millepede** _____ feet; a _____ has four feet.

How many scholars are said to have been involved in the Septuagint, the 3rd century BC Greek translation of the Old Testament? _____

A three cornered figure with equal sides is called an _____ _____ ; . a four sided figure is a _____ .

An _____ is the musical interval between one note and the eighth note above or below in the scale.

Wearing _____ gives soldiers a single appearance; singing in _____ the choristers are all making one sound.

In a _____ competition one player competes with one other at a time; a _____ist supports the existence of more than one culture in society; Esperanto was designed to be a _____ language.

angulus -i m	corner	latus -eris n.	side
annus -i m.	year	pars partis f.	part, party
cornu -us n.	horn	pes pedis m.	foot
forma -ae f.	shape, appearance	sonus -i m.	sound

FARRAGO
— an assortment or medley —

Quantity

_____ are *untouched* (whole) numbers, _____ are *broken* ones.

Combining numbers by _____ you reach the _____ or _____ .

Taking (*dragging*) a number away (from *underneath*) another is _____

.

The process of making a number *many-folded* is _____ .

Something *with* many *folds* is _____ .

A document with *two* / *three* copies (*folds*) is in _____ / _____ .

Single-foldedness is _____ ; having *two* faces (*folds*) is _____ .

To do something without end is to do it *ad in*_____ .

The performance of a player (but not a golfer!) which was not *equal*
to his usual standard could be described as somewhat below

_____

addo -ere (additum)	I give to, combine	plico -are (plicatum)	I fold, double up
finio -ire (finitum)	I end	quantus -a -um	how great/much
frango -ere (fractum)	I break	summus -a -um	greatest
integer gra -grum	untouched	totus -a -um	whole
par paris	equal	traho -ere (tractum)	I drag

Beer and Kippers

Even before the Norman conquest, indeed in most instances even
before the Angles and Saxons had settled in Britain, some Latin words had
been borrowed into their Germanic language. Thus some very English
sounding words turn out to have their origins in Latin. See how many can
you identify and underline in the following passage:

> In the kitchen the cook took a pound of kippers from the box and put
> them in the pan with some pepper and six ounces of peas from a sack. A
> three inch candle stood on the chest along with a glass of beer, a pear and
> some cheap cheese on a tile.

(Check by looking up the following words in the vocabulary at the
back of the book: *bibo, buxus, candela, caseum, caupo, cista, coquus,
culina, cuprum, patina, piper, pirum, pisum, pondo, saccus, tegula and
uncia.*)

You may have included *six*, *three* and *stood* (Latin *sex*, *tres* and *sto*) but these are in fact based on the parallel Germanic version of the same words as the Latin, within the family of linked languages known as Indo-European. You may also have wondered about *glass*: *glaesum* does appear in classical Latin (= amber) but this time it is the borrowing, from the Germanic root from which our modern word is derived!

Inscriptions

Many inscriptions on public buildings and memorials are written in Latin. Here are two examples from Trafalgar Square in London:

on Admiralty Arch, built in public gratitude to Queen Victoria:

> ANNO DECIMO EDWARDI SEPTIMI REGIS
> VICTORIAE REGINAE CIVES GRATISSIMI MDCCCCX
> In the tenth year of King Edward the Seventh
> the citizens most grateful to Queen Victoria 1910

and on the church of St. Martin's in the Fields:

> D. SACRAM AEDEM S. MARTINI PAROCHIANI
> EXSTRUI FEC. A.D. MDCCXXVI
> The parishoners caused (fecerunt) the church of St. (sancti) Martin
> sacred to God (Deo) to be built   A.D. 1726.

Sir Christopher Wren's epitaph is in the crypt of his most famous building, St. Paul's Cathedral:

SUBTUS CONDITUR	Beneath is buried
HUIUS ECCLESIAE ET URBIS CONDITOR	the builder of this church and city
CHRISTOPHORUS WREN,	Christopher Wren,
QUI VIXIT ANNOS ULTRA NONAGINTA,	who lived more than ninety years,
NON SIBI SED BONO PUBLICO.	not for himself but for the public good.
LECTOR, SI MONUMENTUM REQUIRIS,	Reader, if you seek a memorial,
CIRCUMSPICE.	look around

The inscription on one of the buildings of Oriel College, Oxford, records that it was paid for by Cecil Rhodes, the founder of Rhodesia (now Zambia and Zimbabwe). It is also a chronogram, for the capital letters when added together give the date of the building:
MDCCCLLVIIIIII, i.e. _____   (D = 500, L = 50)

e Larga MVnIfICentIa	out of the abundant generosity
CaeCILII rhoDes	of Cecil Rhodes

Look out for Latin inscriptions in your area and make a note of them.

LAST LETTER CLUES

We have seen that English derivatives have often been formed from both the present stem and the supine (or past participle) stem of verbs. Latin verbs show which person is doing the action by changing the final letter(s) instead of requiring a personal pronoun in front of the verb.

'**-o**' shows the agent to be 'I', '**-s**' 'you (singular),
'**-t**' 'he,' 'she' or 'it', '**-mus**' 'we', '**-nt**' 'they'.

Changes in the verb endings are also used to distinguish tenses: thus 'habit*at*' is present, 'plac*ebo*' future and 'affid*avit*' and 'flor*uit*' past.

A number of Latin verb forms are used in English (some of them as nouns now rather than verbs!). The clues above and the main vocabulary will help you to give the literal meaning of the following examples and your dictionary will help you check the English use.

habitat ___*it dwells*___ _*native locality of plant or animal*_

placebo _____ _____

ignoramus _____ _____

aegrotat _____ _____

exeunt _____ _____

affidavit _____ _____

Several words still in use are Latin subjunctives, commanding that something be done: 'let him/it ....'. '-tur' is a passive ending: 'let it be ....'.

fiat _____ _____

exeat _____ _____

habeas corpus_____ _____

imprimatur _____ _____

Latin nouns also change their endings and not only to differentiate singular and plural. The term 'case' is conventionally applied to the different forms used for subject, object and various relationships conveyed by prepositions in English. Latin prepositions are followed by nouns in either the 'accusative' or the 'ablative case'. The 'genitive case' indicates possession or dependence (= 'of') and also contains the full stem of the word which is often more important for English derivatives than the 'nominative' (or subject form). For this reason both cases have been given in the vocabulary. Study the table of common case endings at the top of the next page and then translate the phrases which follow with due attention to the genitive endings.

Table of common noun endings

Nominative (s)	Genitive (s)	Nominative (Pl)	Genitive (Pl)
-a	-ae	-ae	-arum
-us	-i	-i	-orum
-um	-i	-a	-orum
various*	-is	-es/-a	-um

* the full stem of these words is seen in the genitive
N.B. Ablative singulars end in -a, -o, -e and plurals in -is and -ibus.
Look out for these mainly after prepositions in Latin phrases still used in English.

lapsus lingu*ae* _____

modus vivend*i* _____

Zeal Monach*orum* (a village name)_____

dramat*is* personae _____

compos ment*is* _____

in loco parent*is* _____

The word *omnibus* is actually a dative (= 'to/for') plural. How did it come to be used for a public transport vehicle? _____

The word *via* is used in English as an ablative case (= 'by'). "This train will travel to Exeter *via* Newbury and Westbury." _____

Explain the different endings of the Latin word for death in the phrases *post mortem* and *rigor mortis*. _____

The plurals of Latin words in English

Many words which keep their Latin spelling in English have become so naturalized that they are regarded as English and have English plurals. It would seem odd to speak of *arenae, circi, doctores* or *omina*. On the other hand *formulae, termini, appendices* and *genera* are often used as well as English style plurals.. Other words again are only used with their Latin plural terminations — *larvae, stimuli, species, memoranda*. Give the plural form(s) used in English of the following words:

antenna _____ stratum _____ index _____

cactus _____ fungus _____ medium _____

axis _____ vertebra _____ erratum _____

ABBREVIATIONS

brevis = short, brief   abbreviare (late Latin) = to cut short

Many common abbreviations stand for Latin words.   Consider the
following extracts from a biographical index and a personal letter:

> **E.Veryman**— n. A.D.1570, fl. c. 1600
> when he was writing many of his
> books, e.g. *Royal Powers* (jointly with
> A.N. Other — q.v.). For his political
> views v. op. cit. passim, cf. Prof.
> B.L.Ackemall, *The Constitution* chapter
> 7; for posthumous influence v. id. ibid.
> page 349 et seqq.. ob. 1635.

> ...... *I shall be back D.V. on the 3rd prox. and we can
> meet at 11a.m. in town, i.e. at the coffee shop. Pro tem. I
> shall not be using the lawnmower etc. so please make use of
> them ad lib.. N.B. The key to the shed is in the usual place
> viz. under the garden seat..*
>   *Yours, Ursula.*
> *P.S. 4.30p.m. I have just been re-elected nem.con.!!*

Here are the Latin words in full, with space for you to fill in the meanings:

ad libitum	_____	natus	_____
anno domini	_____	nemine contradicente	_____
ante meridiem	_____	nota bene	_____
circa	_____	obiit	_____
confer	_____	opere citato	_____
deo volente	_____	post meridiem	_____
et sequentia	_____	post scriptum	_____
exempli gratia	_____	pro tempore	_____
floruit	_____	proximo (mense)	_____
ibidem	_____	quod vide	_____
id est	_____	vide	_____
idem	_____	videlicet	_____

WORDS AND PHRASES

Many Latin words and phrases are still well used. Some appear on other pages in this book but here are twenty three which you can fit into the appropriate blanks in the passage below. (Each is to be used only once)

ad hoc — for this purpose. special	modus operandi — way of working
ad nauseam — to a disgusting extent	per annum — by the year, annual
crux — critical point (cross)	quid pro quo — compensation (some-
de facto — actually, inreality	thing for something)
de iure — rightfully, lawfully	quondam — some-time, former(ly)
ex officio — by virtue of one's office	quorum — number needed for valid
ex tempore — off-hand, without notes	meeting (of whom)
honorarium — payment for service	sine die — indefinitely (without a day)
in camera — in a judge's private room	sine qua non — indispensible condition
(vault)	(without which not)
in perpetuum — for ever	status quo — present situation (position at
incognito — in disguise (unknown)	which)
inter alia — among other things	terminus ante quem — limit before which
interim — temporary, provisional	verbatim — word for word

Decision Deferred after Secret Plea

Giving his _____ judgement and speaking ___ _____. the judge said that he could not support the _____ _____ . After quoting _____ from his own previous judgements _____ _____ . he said that the _____ of the matter was whether or not a _____ chairman was ___ _____ entitled to an _____ _____ seat on the board ____ _____ as a _____ _____ _____ for the loss of the _____ paid to the chairman ____ _____ . The defendant had argued ____ _____ that such an arrangement was a necessary ____ ____ _____ to maintain the _____ at board meetings. The judge considered this at best an ___ _____ arrangement and doubted whether it was indeed a proper _____ _____ .

However, after a further hearing ____ _____ and representations from the head of MI5, who had slipped into the building _____ , the judge postponed _____ ____ his decision as to the _____ _____ ____ the defendant must give up his ____ _____ seat on the board.

DEBIT AND CREDIT

debitum = something owed   creditum = something entrusted

fiscus — a (money) chest, and in particular the
    emperor's treasury.   *fiscal =*_____
stipendium — a soldier's pay and was then
    also a year's military service. *stipend =* _____
auditus — a hearing. Originally accounts
    were checked by oral recitation. *audit =* _____

Why is the symbol for a pound sterling (£) a form of capital L? _____

At what sort of sale does the price keep increasing?   _____

If some one has little or no money he is   *im*_____

A debtor without the money to 'undo' his debts is   *in*_____

The money paid for the use of money lent (_____) is what 'matters'

    to the lender, provided the 'original' sum (_____) is

    _____ (causing no worry).

Look at the inscription on the obverse of a current
    British coin. What do the letters stand
    for and mean?

_____

_____

    The words ***decus et tutamen*** were originally applied by the Roman poet
Virgil to a breastplate given by Aeneas as a prize to be "an embellishment
(for the man) and a protection (in war)" (Aeneid V, 262) Where can you
find the words inscribed today?

_____

    Nemo me impune lacessit — the motto of the Scottish kings and the
Order of the Thistle. What else is distinctive about the coins on which these
words appear?

_____

augeo (auctum)	I increase	lacesso	I provoke
decus	embellishment	libra	pound
defensor	defender	nemo	no one
fidei (genitive)	of the faith	pecunia	money
gratia (ablative)	by the grace	principalis	first, original, chief
impune	with impunity	securus	free from care
interest	it matters, makes	solvo	I undo, pay
	a difference	tutamen	protection

HORTICULTURE

hortus = garden   colo = I cultivate

_____ = growing crops in fields

viticulture   = _____

arboriculture   = _____

A **carnation** is so called because its flowers are _____ coloured.
The **gladiolus** was so named because its long, stiff
    and pointed leaves were thought to resemble a _____
    (Latin: *gladius*).
The *genus* **campanula** is called after the _____ shape of its flowers
    (late Latin: *campana*).
The *genus* **cineraria** is named from the _____ coloured down on its
    greyish leaves (Latin: *cinis -eris*).
What is the difference between *annuals*, *biennials* and *perennials*?

_____

What qualities would you expect to find in plant varieties distinguished as:

sanguinea	_____	aurea	_____
robusta	_____	ramosa	_____
angustifolia	_____	latifolia	_____
formosa	_____	spinosa	_____
odorata	_____	foetida	_____
speciosa	_____	dentata	_____

Why is the Old Testament quotation *ex spinis uvas* a particularly apt motto
    for Bristol Grammar School founded by wine-merchant Robert Thorne?

_____

ager agri m.	field	forma ae f.	beauty
angustus -a -um	narrow	latus -a -um	broad
annus -i m.	year	odor oris m.	smell
arbor -oris f.	tree	ramus -i m.	branch
aurum -i n.	gold	robur -oris n.	strength
caro carnis f.	flesh, meat	sanguis -inis m.	blood
dens dentis m.	tooth	spina -ae f.	thorn
foetidus -a -um	foul (smelling), noisome	uva -ae f.	grape
folium -ii n.	leaf	vitis -is f.	vine

DOWN YOUR WAY

Most of our English place names originated in the Old English of the Angle Saxon period with Celtic and Scandinavian inclusions but do any of your loc: villages have names which include Latin words? A surprisingly large number d. These often date from medieval times when records were kept in Latin. In th examples which follow you should note the significance of the Latin word(s) in th space provided.

Sometimes the Latin word is an adjective of which the most common are *Magn* or *Parva*. There are neighbouring villages differentiated in this way called *Thornha* in Suffolk, and there are three pairs in Leicestershire alone; sometimes one occu1 without the other:

e.g.   Hutton **Magna** in County Durham   _____

Ruston **Parva** in Humberside   _____

Stow **Longa** in Cambridgeshire   _____

Marston **Sicca** in Glamorgan   _____

St. Columb **Major**}   _____
St. Columb **Minor**} in Cornwall   _____

Rickinghall **Superior**}   _____
Rickinghall **Inferior**}   in Suffolk   _____

Sometimes the Latin word is a genitive noun (= 'of'), giving the owner or patron of the village, or some other association:

e.g.   Rowley **Regis** in West Midlands   _____

Collingbourne **Ducis** in Wiltshire   _____

Ashby **Puerorum** in Norfolk   _____

Buckland **Monachorum** in Devon   _____

Ampney **Crucis** in Gloucestershire   _____

Wick **Episcopi** in Worcestershire   _____

Sutton **Montis** in Somerset   _____

A religious link similar to some of the above is also indicated by the use of th medieval Latin **Abbas** (abbot) and **Prior** (where the village was held by a priory: e.g. Itchen Abbas in Hampshire, Berrick Prior in Oxfordshire.

Prepositions are sometimes used to indicate locality:

e.g.   Weston-**Super-Mare** in Avon   _____

Westbury-**Sub**-Mendip in Somerset   _____

Bradwell-**Juxta**-Coggeshall in Essex   _____

A large number of place names use the element caster/cester/chester from the O English 'ceaester' denoting an old Roman town or fortification (Latin *castra* : military camp).   *Chester* itself was once the Roman legionary fortress of Dev:

mong compound forms of the name are *Manchester* and *Colchester*, which preserve
e Old English pronunciation; *Alcester* in Warwickshire and *Towcester* in
orthamptonshire are two of many using the Anglo-Norman spelling; and *Wroxeter* in
hropshire gives yet another spelling (x =ks).

The Romans built a network of fine roads (*strata viarum* — the laid surfaces of
ads). In Old English the often impressive remains of a Roman road were called
traet' and this has given rise to place names with the element Strat-/ Stret-/ -street etc.,
g. *Stratford, Stretton on Fosse.* The *Fosse* was the name later given to the Roman
ad running from Devon NE to Lincoln (Latin *fossa* = ditch); a number of places
ong the route of the road include the word *Fosse* in their names, e.g. *Street on the
osse* in Somerset.

The Romano-British town names were lost and replaced in the succeeding period
at some at least are revived to-day as names for the archaeological sites or even for
cal estates, shopping precincts or private houses. Where are:

levum _____   Eboracum _____   Aquae Sulis _____

indum _____   Corinium _____   Verulamium _____

Here is a map of Dorset showing the names of Latin interest which can be found in
ne county. Make a similar map of your own county or **vicinity**.

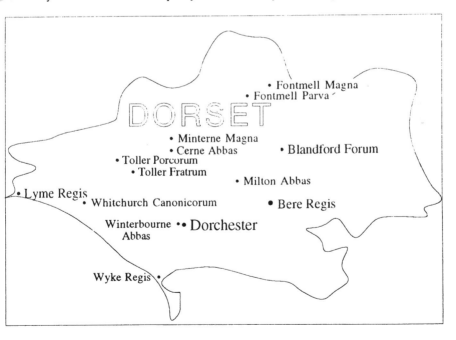

MEMBRA CORPORIS

Various parts of the body are labelled in Latin in the pictures below. Use these Latin words to help you to find the right English words to complete the spaces in the exercise on the opposite page. The clues refer to the appropriate part of the body.

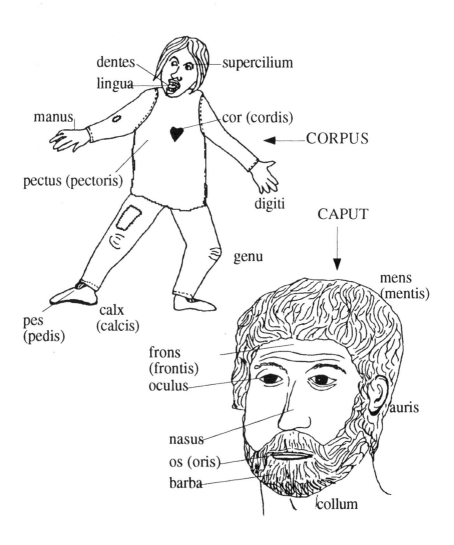

_____ a lever worked by the foot.

_____ work (etc.) done with the hands.

_____ one skilled in different tongues.

_____ clothing, a band etc., worn around the neck.

_____ can be counted on the fingers.

_____ he/she looks after your teeth.

_____ a specialist in diseases of the eyes.

_____ activity, illness etc. of the mind rather than the body.

_____ a greeting (for instance) of this kind comes from the heart.

_____ this kind of test assesses the ear's capacity to discriminate musical notes.

_____ of a test, spoken; of a medicine, taken by mouth.

_____ bulky of body.

_____ this kind of punishment involves loss of head, or life.

_____ this kind of congestion is relieved by a remedy suitable for a blocked nose.

_____ a formally appointed body of persons (e.g. a municipal council).

_____ a country's forehead as it were, or leading boundary.

_____ he trims your beard as well as your hair.

_____ showing contempt with an arrogant arching of the eyebrows.

_____ to bend the knee, e.g. before a religious picture or symbol.

_____ an object, such as a bishop's cross, worn on the chest.

_____ unco-operative, kicking back with the heel.

WHAT IS MY LINE?

The answers to the following clues are all English nouns which are based on the present participles of Latin verbs. (In some cases the appropriate prefix must be added to the simple verb given in the vocabulary.)

The Latin present participle stem ends in -ANT, -ENT or -IENT; the equivalent English present participle (or verbal adjective) ending is -ING.

e.g. exspectare	to look out for	exspectant-	looking out for
permanere	to stay fixed	permanent-	staying fixed

I am growing up

_____

I am suffering, in a hospital perhaps

_____

I am pursuing my academic work with enthusiasm

_____

I am living in this place

_____

I am placing (myself) in your way as rival or enemy

_____

I am sitting apart and opposing the regime

_____

I am ruling, in place of a young prince perhaps

_____

I am answering

_____

I am too young to speak

_____

I am sitting in front (in charge of a nation?)

_____

I am sticking (as a supporter of party or policy?)

_____

I am acting for somebody

_____

I am rising up against those in power

_____

I am in possession of a house (etc.)

_____

I am a (young) offender

_____

adolesco -ere	I mature	patior pati	I suffer
ago -ere	I act	pono -ere	I place
delinquo -ere	I do wrong	rego -ere	I rule
for fari	I speak	respondeo -ere	I answer
habito -are	I live	sedeo -ere (-sid-)	I sit
haereo -ere	I stick	studeo -ere	I am eager, support
occupo -are	I take possession of	surgo -ere	I rise up

IN QUO NEGOTIO VERSOR?

English derivatives from the stem of these Latin nouns will give you a clue as to each person's occupation. In the Latin words in brackets each person says what he or she does, thus providing you with another clue.

medicus _____ (aegros sano)

agricola _____ (agros colo)

custos (custodis) _____ (captivos custodio)

scriptor _____ (libros scribo)

regina _____ (ipsa rego aut uxor sum regis)

miles (militis) _____ (bellum gero; pro patria pugno))

pugil _____ (manibus pugno)

eques _____ (in equo vehor)

pastor _____ (oves curo)

fur _____ (bona aliena furtim capio)

nauta _____ (in nave navigo).

gubernator _____ (navem dirigo aut rempublicam rego)

pauper _____ (nihil pecuniae habeo)

iudex _____ (in iudicio sceleratos condemno)

tiro _____ (miles novus sum)

sacerdos _____ (dis sacrifico et templa curo)
(sacerdotis)

vigil _____ (nocte castra aut urbem custodio)

arbiter _____ (inter disputantes iudico)

OBLIGATION
ligo -are = I bind

Latin verbs add a special ending (**-and/-end**) to show that the action of the verb must be done.   A number of these Latin obligation words are in common use in English.   If one thing is to be done the final ending will be **-um**, whereas the neuter plural and the feminine singular both end in **-a**. Several English words have dropped the adjectival ending altogether and two musical terms borrowed from Italian end in **-o**.

_____	a list of things to be done, or discussed by a committee.
_____	a note of something to be borne in mind, remembered.
_____	a list of things to be added.
_____	a list of errors to be put right.
_____	putting a question which is to be sent back to the whole body of voters for decision.
_____	a girl's name: she is to be loved.
_____	a girl's name: she is to be wondered at or admired.
_____	the portion to be distributed, e.g. to share-holders.
_____	a non-historical story, 'to be read'.
_____	to be played with increasing loudness.
_____	to be played with lessening loudness.

What is meant by the words **mutatis mutandis**?
   e.g. The death of Tito and subsequent decline of a central dictatorship led to an increasing desire for indepedence among the 'republics' which comprised Yugoslavia;   this was quickly followed by conflict between the different nationalities.   The same was true, *mutatis mutandis*, in the Soviet Union.

addo	I add	divido	I separate, share out
ago	I do, discuss	lego	I read
amo	I love	memoro	I recall
corrigo	I put straight	miror	I wonder at, admire
cresco	I increase	muto	I change
diminuo	I lessen	refero	I take back, refer to

LITIGATION

ius iuris = a right   lis litis = a lawsuit   lex legis = a law

In these extracts. from reports by our legal correspondent. underline the words which have their origins in Latin (the general vocabulary will help you with the root words and their meanings) and give the meanings of the actual Latin words and phrases which have been included.

Testimony doubted

In concluding his summing up the judge admonished the jury not to be prejudiced by reports which had illegally appeared in the media while the matter was still *sub judice*. The *prima facie* case against the defendant rested on the suggestion that he had been seen *in flagrante delicto*. His lordship questioned the *bona fides* of the prosecution witness, who had previous convictions for perjury and who had first reported the crime to the police under an *alias*. The jury had heard the defendant's convincing *alibi* and should also note the absence of any forensic evidence.

Maker to blame — faulty product banned

In granting an injunction against further disposal of the goods in question the judge ruled that it was not a matter of *caveat emptor* when the manufacturer's culpable negligence had clearly breached the terms of his licence.

Validity of will questioned

The legacies detailed in a codicil to the deceased's will were very laudable but, during the inquest, the coroner doubted whether the testator was still *compos mentis* by the date of the will. Furthermore the solicitor involved had since been served a *sub poena* to give evidence in a case of serious fraud.

sub judice = _____

prima facie = _____

in flagrante delicto = _____

bona fides = _____

alias = _____

alibi = _____

caveat emptor = _____

compos mentis = _____

sub poena = _____

BUILDING WORDS FROM TWO STEMS

Using the vocabulary to help, complete the spaces below with the English words, based on a combination of two Latin stems, which have the given meanings. Several of these words were combined like this by the Romans themselves but others are more recent inventions. You will need to use most of the words in the vocabulary several times but some of them will appear in English in more than one form.

aequus (equi-)	equal	lex (legis)	law
ambo	both	loquor (locut-)	I speak
bellum	war	male	badly
bene	well	manus	hand
caedo (cidium)	I kill (a killing)	nox	night
caro (carn-)	meat, flesh	omnis	all, every
circum	around	paene (pen-)	almost
cura	care, attention	panis	bread
dexter	right	potens (potent-)	powerful
dico (dict-)	I say, speak	scio (scient-)	I know
facio (fact-)	I make, do	scribo (script-)	I write, draw
fero (lat- !!)	I carry, bear	spicio (spect-)	I look
frater	brother	sui	of oneself
gero	I wage, conduct	valeo (valent-)	I am strong, of value,
grandis	great, pompous		fare well
herba	grass	venter	stomach
homo	human being	vice	in turn, instead of
insula	island	volo (volent-)	I wish
ius (iuris)	right, law	voro	I devour, eat

_____ a document written by hand

_____ a narrow promontary, almost an island

_____ round-about speech

_____ of like worth

_____ well-wishing, kindly

_____ killing one's brother

_____ somebody who does good

_____ I draw around, delimit

_____ making things (originally) by hand labour

_____ a speaking well, blessing

39

_____ feeding on all kinds of food

_____ a saying farewell

_____ killing a fellow human being

_____ able to use both hands equally

_____ cautious, one who has looked all round

_____ a speaking badly, cursing, a curse

_____ treatment of the hands

_____ eating grass and plants

_____ knowing everything

_____ an evil doer

_____ speaking in a lofty or pompous way

_____ with arguments/evidence of equal value both ways

_____ wishing ill towards

_____ eating flesh

_____ killing oneself

_____ time when night and day are of the same length

_____ waging war, aggressive

_____ the carrying or passing of laws

_____ chemical killing grass and other non-woody plants

_____ all powerful

_____ one with whom you share (use prefix 'com-') bread

_____ exercise or declaration of judicial authority

_____ periphery, boundary carried round

_____ one who conducts (government) on another's behalf

_____ one speaking in such a way that the sound seems
to come from elsewhere (literally, 'belly-speaker')

CAELESTIAL REGIONS

avis	bird	regio -ionis	district, region
caelum	sky, heaven	satelles -itis	attendant
fulmino	I lighten, thunder	sol	sun
luna	moon	stella	star

Why were early aeroplane pilots called **aviators**? _____

What is: a **constellation**? _____ a **satellite**? _____

What is the English name for **Ursa Maior**? _____

He **fulminated** against dictatorship. What did he do? _____

Fill in the Latin names which we still use for the signs of the Zodiac in the grid
below and add the English translations (the main vocabulary will help).

DEITIES

Apart from the earth, the planets in our solar system have been named after
;raeco-)Roman gods (or in one case, a goddess). Complete the mythological family
:e below with the names of the planets.

```
┌──────────┐
│          │= Ge (Earth)
└──────────┘
      ┌──────────┐
      │          │= Rhea        (The Titans)
      └──────────┘
 Juno (1)=┌──────────┐  ┌──────────┐  ┌──────────┐
          └──────────┘  └──────────┘  └──────────┘
┌──────────┐
└──────────┘
 Maia  (2)=│
           │
 ┌──────────┐
 └──────────┘
         Dione(3)=│
           ┌──────────┐
           └──────────┘
```

Astrologers believe that people's characters are affected by the planets. Which
:avenly body is supposed to be influencing somebody who is

▸vial _____   warlike _____   lunatic _____

; changeable as quicksilver _____ ?

(ost days of our week are named after Norse gods: which day is named after one of
.e Roman gods in the genealogy above?   _____   What sort of character
is been associated with this planet?   _____

Some of the other planets besides the earth have their own "moons". The names
.ven to these have often been chosen to be mythologically appropriate. Which
.anets are orbited by:

:haron _____   Nereid _____   Titan _____

▸ _____   Rhea _____   Europa _____

Explain the words in italics in relation to figures in Graeco-Roman mythology:
fter his *bacchic* indulgence the night before, breakfast *cereal* had little appeal.

_____

_____

fter his *herculean* effort rowing the *Atlantic*, he planned to explore *volcanoes*.

_____

_____

SCIENCE

What is *science*?   Much scientific vocabulary has links with Latin. Consider for instance the words in italics in the following sentences:

> After the *apparatus* had been used to *conduct experiments* the *results* were *computed* and a *conclusion produced* in the shape of a new *formula*.

> These *data* concerning *supersonic velocities* help us to *calculate* the *acceleration* needed to break out of *gravity induced* earth *orbit* and *explore* the *infinity* of *space*.

> Brine *solution* was heated in a flask to *vaporize* it; the cooling vapour *condensed* and *formed* drops of *distilled* water; *salt* and other *impurities* were left in the flask.

What are *elements*?

_____

compound substances?

_____

_____

What about *Tellurium*?

Many more recently discovered elements have been given names based on Greco-Roman mythology: e.g. Uranium, Plutonium, Titanium, Promethium, Neptunium.   Helium and Selenium are Greek names connecting those elements to the sun and moon.

_____

The chemical symbols used for several of the more familiar elements are based on their Latin names. Which substances do the following symbols signify?

Fe _____   Au _____   Pb _____

C _____   Ag _____   Ca _____

What is the name for a scientist's 'work' room?   _____

What is the term for 'cutting apart' specimens?   _____

Where do *metals* come from?   _____

What occurs when soil is 'eaten away' (e.g. by water)?   _____

What kind of bridge is 'hung under' cables?   _____

What device 'heaps up' a generated electrical charge? _____

A simple tool for 'lifting' or moving an object? _____

The name for 'hidden' heat needed to change a
   substance from one state to another
   without raising its temperature? _____

What is the term for separating a substance
   from contact with others, as an 'island'? _____

What names are given for the transfer of heat when
   it spreads out as 'rays'? _____
   it is 'guided' from one substance to
         another in contact with it? _____
   it 'travels with' the currents set up in a
         volatile substance such as air? _____

What is the link between 'pebbles' and computers? _____

What is the difference between
   igneous and *sedimentary* rocks? _____

   nuclear *fission* and *fusion*? _____

What are the stages of the cycle of a 4 stroke *combustion* engine?

1) 'throwing in' fuel _____   2) 'squashing together' _____

3) 'firing' _____   4) 'draining off' fumes _____

argentum	silver	inicio (iniectum)	I throw in
aurum	gold	insula	island
calculus	pebble	laboro (laboratum)	I work
calx calcis	limestone	lateo	I am hidden
carbo	charcoal	levo (levis)	I lift (light)
compono	I put together	metallum	mine
cumulus	pile, heap	plumbum	lead
do (datum)	I give	puto	I think
duco (ductum)	I lead, guide	radius	ray
elementum	letter, rudiment	scientia	knowledge
erodo (erosum)	I gnaw out	seco (sectum)	I cut
exhaurio (-stum)	I drink off, drain	sedimentum (sedeo)	settlement (I sit)
ferrum	iron	substantia (substo)	matter (stand under)
findo (fissum)	I split	suspendo (-sum)	I hang under
fundo (fusum)	I pour, melt	tellus telluris	earth
ignis	fire	vehor (vectus)	I travel

# MEDICAL BULLETIN
medicus = doctor

bulla = a small box, containing a charm, worn round the neck by Roman children.   Then it came to mean a seal and hence a document given under seal, especially a papal 'bull'.   The diminutive forms used in Italian and then French came to mean 'a short report'; hence 'bulletin' in English.

Many medical terms and the names given to parts of the body in particular are Latin or modelled on Latin.

Which part of the body is called a 'two-headed little mouse'?   _____

Which bodily organs are called 'acorns'?   _____

Which bones have names meaning 'basin' and 'broach'?   _____

What is the name for hairlike blood vessels?   _____

and for those carrying blood back to the heart?   _____

Which part is affected if the patient has: *cerebral* palsy?   _____

pulmonary inflammation?   _____

Remedia

_____   medicine 'thrown into' the patient

_____   'work' undertaken on the patient's body

_____   machine to bring moving air into patient's lungs

_____   medicine in a little 'ball'

_____   medicine in a little 'box'

_____   medicine for the patient to drink

_____   piercing the patient with needles

_____   preparation for diabetes made from 'islands' of special small cells found in the pancreas of animals

_____   soft mass (originally damp bread) applied to soothe wound)

_____   originally a 'walking' hospital accompanying an army; now a vehicle taking patients to a hospital.

_____   originally a refuge for the infirm or destitute where there was a 'host' to look after them.

_____   a place for healing invalids.

Fill in the gaps in the following:

_____ staff help the doctors, nurses and other professional workers in the health service. A person with an _____ disease is liable to taint the air around him with germs, but a _____ disease is spread by direct physical contact. We _____ instruments etc. to make them 'barren', free from bacteria etc. which could otherwise multiply and harm the patient.

_____ : to implant disease germs in a person to enable him to develop *immunity*; the word was originally a metaphor from gardening meaning to graft or put in an 'eye' (=bud).

_____ : modified *virus* for use in the above procedure, originally of cowpox and so named from the word for 'cow'.

acus -us f. needle		oculus -i m.	eye
ambulo -are	I walk	operor -ari -atus	I work on
ancilla -ae f.	maid	pelvis -is f.	basin
biceps (cf. caput)	two-headed	pila (dimin. pilula)	ball
capillus -i m.	a hair	potio -ionis f.	drink, draught
capsa (dimin. capsula)	box	pulmo -onis m.	lung
cerebrum -i n.	brain	puls pultis f.	thick pottage
contagio -ionis f.	touching	pungo (punctum)	I pierce, prick
contingo (contactum)	I touch	remedium -ii n.	cure
fibula -ae f.	pin, clasp	sano -are	I heal
gans glandis f.	acorn	sterilis -e	barren
hospes hospitis	host, friend	vacca -ae f.	cow
inficio (infectum)	I dip in, dye, stain	vena -ae f.	vein
mus muris m.	mouse	ventus -i m.	wind

Roman surgical instruments found in a house in Pompeii

# GOVERNMENT
gubemo = I steer, direct, rule

Political Parties — What do their names suggest?

a) _____ — representing the working class

b) _____ — preserving the existing situation

c) _____ — absolute authority associated with the Roman consuls

d) _____ — collective ownership of property

e) _____ — the generous spirit of the free man

f) _____ — community control over production and distribution of resources

g) _____ — a state belonging to its citizens, the public

Types of Governments

a) _____ administers   a particular place

b) _____   a town

c) _____   those who identify as a group forming a distinct country

d) _____   political communities linked by a treaty

e) _____   an empire

communis e	common, public	locus -i m.	place
conservo - are	I preserve	municipium	self-governing town
foedus -eris n.	treaty, alliance	natio -ionis	tribe, people
imperium -ii n.	power, empire	respublica	common weal, state
laboro -are	I work	socius -ii m.	ally
liber -a -um	free	socialis -e	belonging to allies
liberalis -e	befitting a free man	societas -atis	alliance, community

candidus: white; *candidatus*: a man seeking office wore specially whitened toga,.
fasces: bundles of rods and axes carried before consul as symbols of authority.
patricii: the original Roman nobility of birth; later *plebeians* (members of the *plebs* = lower classes) too were enobled by holding the consulship.
plebiscitum: decree of the common people (*plebs*); acquired force of a law.
proletarii: lowest citizens serving state with not property but children (*proles*).
rostrum: beak (of ship); prows of captured ships formed a platform in the *forum*.
triumphus: a victorious general's splendid procession into Rome to the Capitol.

47

The following passage demonstrates the range and extent of Latin based words in our political vocabulary. Underline the Latin based words and consider their meanings and derivations. Some words are given in the vocabularies on these pages; others have been encountered already and may be checked in the general vocabulary at the back of the book.

Rex Valery, 1st Duke of Vectis

Rex Valery came from humble origins and it was his eloquent oratory from the conference rostrum, denouncing nepotism and defending proletarian liberties, which first attracted popular attention. Adopted by his local constituency party as their candidate, he was soon elected by a massive majority. Rapidly elevated to Minister and then Secretary of State, with a clear mandate to introduce radical reforms in urban and rural administration, he brought in legislation which was lauded as a triumph of civic constitutional progress.

Rex was subsequently created Duke by Her Majesty and joined the hereditary nobility, but his plebeian spirit could not be reconciled to their patrician conventions any more than to the pomp and regalia of state occasions. Yet he was a firm supporter of bicameral government and so he now proposed that his future colleagues should be appointed to office by universal suffrage for a limited term. This suggestion was rejected in a plebiscite and Rex, despite the pleas of his associates, went into retirement declaring, "*vox populi est suprema lex.*"

civis is	citizen	opto -are	I choose
collega -ae m.	partner in office	orator -is (oro)	pleader, speaker (I beg)
constituo (-tutum)	I set up, appoint,	origo -inis f.	origin. beginning
creo -are	I elect, appoint	partes partium	a party, faction
denuntio -are	I give notice	pompa -ae f.	solemn procession
heres heredis	heir	populus -i m.	people. nation
humilis -e	humble	regalis -e	belonging to a king
libertas -tatis f.	freedom	rus ruris n.	the countryside
mandatum -i n.	instruction	suffragium -ii n.	vote
massa -ae f.	lump, mass	supremus -a -um	highest, final
minister -tri m.	servant	urbs urbis f.	city
nepos nepotis m.	grandson, relative	Vectis	Isle of Wight
officium -ii n.	duty	vox vocis f.	voice

WATCH THAT SPELLING

-tion or -sion?

Words ending in *-tion* or *-sion* are derived from Latin or Late Latin nouns in *-io* which themselves are based on the supine stem (see page 12) of related verbs. After the letters 'c' and 'p' the ending is *-Tion*, e.g. *action*, *inscription* and very many others. A small number of words have double 'ss', e.g. *mission* (mitto), *confession* (confiteor), *session* (sedeo), *oppression* (-premo), *concussion* (concutio). Other words are less predictable: look up the Latin verb in the general vocabulary and check whether its supine has 's' or 't' to help you in filling in the missing letter in the following words.

e.g. posi_t_ion   _place where thing was put_   (pono positum = I place, put)

tradi_ion _____
(trado — I hand over)

provi_ion _____
(pro + video — I see)

deri_ion _____
(de + rideo — I laugh at, scorn)

inci_ion _____
(in + caedo — I cut)

peti_ion _____
(peto — I seek)

audi_ion _____
(audio — I hear)

conven_ion _____
(con + venio — I come)

ascen_ion _____
(ascendo = ad + scando — I climb)

man_ion _____
(maneo — I remain)

dissen_ion _____
(dis + sentio — I feel)

reten_ion _____
(re + teneo — I hold)

pen_ion _____
(pendo — I weigh out, pay)

comprehen_ion _____
(cum + prehendo — I grasp)

conver_ion _____
(con + verto — I turn)

solu_ion _____
(solvo — I undo)

fu_ion _____
(fundo — I pour)

delu_ion _____
(de + ludo — I play)

elocu_ion _____
(e + loquor — I speak)

constitu_ion _____
(constituo = cum + statuo — I set up)

exclu_ion _____
(ex + claudo — I shut)

sta_ion _____
(sto — I stand)

occa_ion _____
(ob + cado — I fall)

occupa_ion _____
(occupo = ob + capio — I take over)

persua_ion _____
(per + suadeo — I urge)

conversa_ion _____
(con + versor — I engage in)

inva_ion _____
(in + vado — I go)

mo_ion _____
(moveo — I move)

adhe_ion _____
(ad + haereo — I stick)

dele_ion _____
(deleo— I destroy, remove)

saluta_ion _____
(saluto — I greet)

expul_ion _____
(ex + pello — I drive)

explo_ion _____
(ex + plaudo — I clap out, drive off)

comple_ion _____
(compleo — I fill)

le_ion _____
(laedo — I hurt)

-able or -ible?

Latin formed many adjectives by adding -abilis to the stem of first conjugation verbs (those with an infinitive ending in -are) and -ibilis to the stem of other verbs. More such words were formed in late and medieval Latin and either directly or through French these have come into English as adjectives ending in -ble. You can check whether the preceding vowel, in English as in Latin, is 'a' or 'i' by looking up the simple Latin verb in the main vocabulary and noting whether or not it is first conjugation.

e.g. indubita ble *not to be doubted* (dubito dubitare = I doubt)

laud_ble _____
(laudo — I praise)

leg_ble _____
(lego— I read)

tang_ble _____
(tango— I touch)

mut_ble _____
(muto— I change)

cred_ble _____
(credo— I believe)

navig_ble _____
(navigo— I sail)

culp_ble _____
(culpo— I blame)

irrevoc_ble _____
(voco — I call)

convert_ble _____
(verto— I turn)

insuper_ble _____
(supero— I overcome)

invinc_ble _____
(vinco— I conquer)

aud_ble _____
(audio— I hear)

excit_ble _____
(cito— I rouse)

admir_ble _____
(miror— I wonder at)

50

Watch that spelling (cont.)

ed_ble _____
(edo— I eat)

vulner_ble _____
(vulnero— I wound)

horr_ble _____
(horreo— I bristle, am alarmed)

habit_ble _____
(habito— I live)

fall_ble _____
(fallo— I deceive)

elig_ble _____
(eligo = e + lego — I choose)

resist_ble _____
(resisto— I stand up to)

terr_ble _____
(terreo— I frighten)

dur_ble _____
(duro— I make hard, endure)

inexor_ble _____
(in + ex + oro— I beg)

implac_ble _____
(placo— I appease)

compar_ble _____
(cum + paro — I prepare)

deplor_ble _____
(ploro— I lament)

indel_ble _____
(deleo— I destroy)

intract_ble _____
(in + tracto— I handle, manage)

indisput_ble _____
(in + dis + puto — I think)

delect_ble _____
(delecto— I delight)

indel_ble _____
(deleo— I destroy)

It is interesting to note that many of the Latin adjectives had active as well as passive meanings: e.g. *vincibilis = conquering* or *conquerable*. Almost all the English words have a passive meaning: did you spot the few exceptions?

Similar adjectives have also been formed from the supine stem of many verbs (e.g. *visible, sensible, admissible*). Late Latin formed such adjectives based on nouns or even existing adjectives (e.g. *amicus — friend: amicabilis, amicable; capax (capio) — able to hold: capabilis, capable*). English has coined a very large number of new adjectives, for which there are no Latin equivalents, in *-able* on both Latin and non-Latin stems (e.g. *creditable, , movable; eatable, saleable, agreeable*).

-ant or -ent?

The following English adjectives are based on Latin present participles (see page 34). The vowel in the ending depends upon the conjugation of the Latin verb: check in the vocabulary and if the infinitive ends in *-are* the participle too will have 'a' rather than 'e'.

e.g. **vigil_a_nt** being watchful (vigilo -are = I am awake, keep watch)

toler_nt	_____	leni_nt	_____
perman_nt	_____	disson_nt	_____
milit_nt	_____	praecipit_nt	_____
repugn_nt	_____	abhorr_nt	_____
ard_nt	_____	triumph_nt	_____
expedi_nt	_____	afflu_nt	_____
err_nt	_____	ignor_nt	_____
dist_nt	_____	intermitt_nt	_____
emolli_nt	_____	deterr_nt	_____

Where the last letter before the -_nt ending is 'c' or 'g' the pronunciation gives a useful clue: the letters are pronounced soft (i.e. as 's' and 'j') before 'e' but remain hard ('g' and 'k') before 'a'.

cog_nt	_____	extravag_nt	_____
pung_nt	_____	resurg_nt	_____
vac_nt	_____	dec_nt	_____
adjac_nt	_____	retic_nt	_____

There are however some snags: *violent* has an 'e' because it is derived from the Latin adjective *violentus* (rather than the verb *violo -are*). *Sisto* is a 3rd conjugation (*-ere*) verb but English derivatives are *inconsistent* in their choice of vowel: e.g. *subsistence*, but *resistance* and *assistance*.

In old French the *-ant* ending became generalised for all present participles even when the original Latin verb was not 1st conjugation (*-are*) and some of the resulting words have come into English with the *-ant* rather than *-ent* spelling:

e.g. *defendant, attendant, descendant, tenant.*

To add to the confusion some Latinized forms , in *-ent*, were later adopted as well:

e.g. *dependent* (adj.) as well as *dependant* (noun)

Moreover *aparant* became relatinized as *apparent*. On the other hand *confident* (adj.) was **later** joined by *confidant* (noun) after the pronunciation of the later French word *confidente*.

WORD PLAY

Choose a Latin word and a related theme; then see how many English derivatives you can introduce into a short paragraph. Here are some suggestions:

All in the Mind?

Although they viewed with *magnanimous equanimity* the *animism* which so *animated* the lives of those among whom they were now living, there could be no *pusillanimous* acceptance of a *mentality* which assigned religious veneration to the *inanimate*; the latter they *unanimously* regarded as *demented*.

animus = mind, spirit
mens mentis = mind

Hang up?

The *propensity* of his *appendix* to erupt kept him in perpetual *suspense* regarding an *impending* operation. He *pensively pondered* a medical *compendium* and, *pending* a decision on calling the doctor, *dispensed* himself a dose of the *expensive* brandy on which he regularly, albeit unwisely *depended* to restore his *poise*.

pendeo = I hang
pendo = I weigh
pondus -eris = weight

Last Breath?

Despite his *respiratory* difficulties it was Spiro's unflagging *spirit* which *inspired* the *conspirators* to keep working at a *sprightly* pace until their limbs ran with *perspiration*. When, however, it *transpired* that their *spiritual* leader had actually *expired*, their own *aspirations* faded quickly.

spiro -are = I breathe
spiritus = breath, spirit

Not such a Push-over!

A sudden *impulse* to *dispel* his *pulsating* head-ache and have done with the *repulsive* boy once and for all *propelled* Mr. Driver to the point of *expelling* him forthwith. The latter, however, *repelled* by the likely results of such a *repulse, compelled* his father to *appeal* to the governors but they felt no *compulsion* to *repeal* the *expulsion* order.

pello (pulsum)= I push

appeal and *repeal* are from the same root via French.

What a follow on!

This *sequence* of events seemed like *persecution* to our *consequential executive*. After so many *consecutive* misfortunes the *subsequent* decision by the *obsequious prosecutor* not to *execute* a summons was but a small respite. In the *sequel* the grief of presiding over his son's *obsequies* and acting as his *executor* resulted in his decision to retire.

sequor sequi secutus sum
I follow

Plain Speaking?

After such an *affable confabulation* with the editor on that fateful day I *confess* that I was not expecting his *prefatory* remarks to be so *ineffably defamatory*, still less that his *infamous preface* would prove *fatal* to himself.

for fari fatus = I speak
confiteor -eri confessus = I admit
fatum = what is said. ordained
fabula = a tale told
fama = talk (of crowd). repute

Broken!

The *fragile* lenses *fractured* at once and the prisms which had *refracted* the sunlight so wonderfully lay in *fragments*. After a moment of stunned silence the child broke into a *refrain* of sobs whose volume belied his own *frail* appearance.

frango fractum = I break

frail came into English from Norman French. *fragile* was introduced later directly from the same original Latin *fragilis*.

Lively Lady

For some days before the *vital viva voce* examination the *surviving* candidates tried to fortify their flagging *vitality* by taking *vitamin* pills with their daily *vitals*. On the day itself the normally *vivacious* Helen, acutely nervous at the prospect, so *vivid* in her imagination, of being asked to defend her views on *vivisection*, tried to *revive* her courage with a fresh carnation for her button-hole.

vivo -ere = I live
vivus = alive
vita = life

Now it is your turn. Use the vocabulary at the back of this book and your English dictionary as you explore the relationships between words which interest you. May your researches prove fruitful and enjoyable!

INDEX OF PROPER NAMES

ROMAN FAMILY AND PERSONAL NAMES
(See *Nomenclature*; some English derivative names are given here in brackets)

Aemilius	family name: *aemulus* = rival, eager. (Emile, Emily, Amelia).
Antonius	family name of uncertain meaning (Anthony, Tony etc.)
Augustus	=revered; title given to Octavian and by which he is best known; subsequently used by following emperors. (Augusta, Austin, Gus etc.)
Caecilius	family name: *caecus* = blind. (Cecil, Cecilia etc.)
Claudius	family name: claudus = lame.
Horatius	family name. (Horace, Horatio).
Julius	family name, perhaps = descended from Jupiter, but see also *Iulus* in the mythology section.
Lucius	first name = of the light.
Marcellus	a diminutive of *Marcus* used as a family name.
Marcus	first name, linked to Mars, god of war.
Paulus	added name = small.
Terentius	family name. (Terence, Terry etc.)
Valerius	family name = strong.

NAMES FROM MYTHOLOGY
(See *Nomenclature* and *Caelestial Regions*. Greek equivalent names are given in brackets.)

Atlas	a Titan (q.v.) who held up the sky on his shoulders and was turned to stone when Perseus showed him the Gorgon's head, becoming the Atlas Mountains in NW Africa.
Bacchus	(also called Dionysus), son of Zeus (=Jupiter) and the Theban princess Semele; god of wine.
Camilla	warrior queen of the Volsci. In Virgil's Aeneid she joins in the fighting in Italy and is killed.
Ceres	(= Demeter) sister of Jupiter and goddess of crops and corn.
Charon	ferryman of the dead across the river Styx in the underworld.
Diana	(= Artemis) goddess of hunting, wild animals and virginity.

Europa	she was beloved by Zeus (= Jupiter) who turned himself into a bull to carry her over the sea.
Ge	Earth, wife of Uranus.
Hercules	(= Heracles) son of Zeus (=Jupiter) and Alcmene, a hero famous for his great strength. Among his exploits were the 12 'Labours'.
Io	a princess beloved by Zeus (= Jupiter) and turned into a cow.
Iulus	son of Aeneas. The Julian family claim to be descended from him is supported in Virgil's Aeneid.
Juno	(= Hera) wife of Jupiter and queen of the gods.
Jupiter	(= Zeus) king of the gods; father of various gods and heroes by a variety of goddesses, nymphs and mortal girls. The Latin genitive form *Iovis* has given us the English expressions 'by Jove' and 'jovial'.
Mars	Son of Jupiter and Juno and god of war. In Roman mythology he was the father of Romulus and Remus and honoured in the name of his month, *mensis Martialis*. The names Marc/k, Marcel(lle) and Martin are all connected with Mars.
Mercurius	(= Hermes) son of Jupiter and the nymph Maia; messenger of the gods and portrayed with winged sandals.
Neptune	(= Poseidon) brother of Jupiter and god of the sea.
Nereid	a sea nymph, daughter of Nereus.
Pluto	(= Hades) brother of Jupiter and god of the underworld.
Rhea	wife (and sister) of Saturn.
Saturnus	(= Cronos) son of Uranus and Ge; father of Jupiter and the gods. Also in Roman mythology the king of Latium during the golden age; his festival, the Saturnalia, was celebrated in mid-winter with feasting and present giving, but being born under the planet Saturn is thought by astrology to give a gloomy disposition.
Titans	the children of Uranus and Ge.
Uranus	Heaven, husband of Ge.
Veus	(= Aphrodite) sometimes said to be the daughter of Zeus (= Jupiter) and Dione, she rose from the sea surf and came ashore near Paphos in Cyprus; goddess of love. The Latin genitive is *Veneris*, hence the use of venereal for sexually transmitted diseases.
Vulcanus	(= Hephaistos) son of Jupiter and Juno and blacksmith of the gods. His forge was believed to be under the vulcano Mount Etna.

VOCABULARY

A few words whose meaning has been given on the page where they occur have not been repeated here, but the vast majority of the words used in the book are included. Compounds however, that is words beginning with a prepositional prefix, are not for the most part given separate entries, although there are some exceptions where these seemed useful: generally the student should look up the simple word and then consider the extra significance of the prefix.

Nouns have been given together with their genitive case (often in full) and gender. Adjectives have been listed with indications of their different gender endings, except for those in the 3rd declension with all genders alike in the nominative case; the genitive of these has been given.

Verbs are nearly all given with their full principal parts (i.e. present tense, infinitive, perfect tense and supine); the supine stem is underlined whenever it gives rise to English derivatives, even if the latter have not been used in the text. In the case of the infinitive usually, and the perfect sometimes, the endings only are given.

The letter 'i' in Latin can represent a consonant ('j') as well as a vowel. When looking for the Latin source of an English word with a 'j' you should look under 'i'. Remember too that in a compound form a vowel 'e' or 'i' may represent a vowel 'a' in the simple word: e.g. reticeo is a compound of taceo — see also p.14. The Latin diphthong 'ae' is often represented in English by a plain 'e': thus *edifice* comes from *aedificium*. The Romans themselves made no distinction in writing between 'u' (vowel) and 'v' (consonant). Latin inscriptions often follow the Roman custom of writing capital 'u' as 'V' — an example is at the bottom of page 23.

absens absentis (absentia -ae f.)	absent (asence)
acus -us f.	needle
ad (preposition + acc.) (ad hoc)	to, towards (for this [purpose])
addo -ere addidi addi̱tum	I add
adolesco -ere adolevi adu̱ltum	I mature
aedes aedis f. (cf. aedificium)	temple (church); house. (building, edifice)
aeger aegra aegrum (aegroto -are)	sick, ill (I am sick)
aequus -a -um (equi-)	equal
affido -are (medieval)	I declare on oath
ager agri m.	field
ago -ere egi a̱ctum	I do, discuss, act
alias adv.	at another time
alibi adv.	in another place
alienus -a -um	belonging to somebody else
alius alia aliud	other, another
altus -a -um (altior)	high, deep (higher)
ambo ae -o	both
ambulo -are	I walk
amo -are	I love
amplus -a -um	copious, large, abundant
ancilla -ae f.	maid, servant
angulus -i m.	corner
angustus -a -um	narrow
animus -i m.	mind, soul, spirit

annus -i m.	year (cf. biennual — with a two year cycle)
ante (preposition + acc.)	before
antenna -ae f.	sail-yard
appareo -ere -ui apparitum	I appear
appendix appendicis m.	that which hangs upon a thing. supplement
aptus -a -um	suitable. fitting
aqua -ae f. (aquarius -ii m.)	water (water-carrier)
arbiter arbitri m.	one who decides. arbitrator
arbor arboris f.	tree
ardeo -ere arsi arsum	I am on fire, blaze
arduus -a -um	steep. difficult
arena -ae f.	sand. arena
argentum -i n.	silver
aries arietis m.	ram
ars artis f.	skill. art, technique
artus -us m. (adj. articulatus -a -um)	joint. limb (jointed)
astrum -i n.	star
auctoritas auctoritatis f.	authority. prestige
audio -ire audivi auditum	I hear. listen to
augeo -ere auxi auctum	I increase
auris auris f.	ear
aurum -i n.	gold
aut	either. or
avis -is f.	bird
axis -is m.	axle. pivot
barba -ae f.	beard
beatus -a -um	happy (*beatric-* = she who makes happy)
bellum -i n.	war
bene adv.	well
bibo -ere (monastic Latin *biber*)	I drink (a drink: old English *beor* = beer)
biceps (cf. caput)	two-headed
bini -ae -a	two at a time
bis adv.	twice
bonus -a -um (bona)	good (goods, possessions)
buxus -i f.	box-tree (the wood was used for boxes)
cactus -i m.	prickly plant
cado (-cido) -ere cecidi casum	I fall
caedo -ere cecidi caesum (-cisum)	I kill (cidium = a killing)
caelum -i n.	sky, heaven
calculus -i m.	pebble, counter
calx calcis f.	heel
calx calcis f.	limestone
camera -ae f.	arch. vault
campana -ae f. (late Latin)	bell
cancer cancri m.	crab
candela -ae f.	wax light, tallow taper, candle
candidus -a -um	shining, bright, white
canto -are -avi cantatum	I sing
caper capri m. (capricornus)	goat (capricorn — having goat horns)
capillus -i m.	a hair
capio -ere cepi captum	I take, capture

capsa -ae f. (dimin. capsula) — box
caput capitis n. — head
carbo carbonis m. — charcoal
carcer carceris m. — prison
caro carnis f. — flesh, meat
carpo -ere carpsi carptum — I pluck, take hold of (cf. *excerpt*)
carus -a -um — dear, beloved
caseus -i m. — cheese (old German *chasi*, old Eng. **ciese*)
castra castrorum n.pl. — military camp
casus -us m. (cf. *cado*) — fall, chance, misfortune, occurrence
caupo cauponis m. — inn-keeper, trader
(old Eng. *ceap* = market; hence *cheap*)
caveo -ere cavi cautum — I take precautions, beware
cedo -ere cessi cessum — I yield, go
celo -are — I hide, conceal
centum — a hundred
cerebrum -i n. — brain
cerno -ere crevi cretum — I distinguish, perceive, decree
certus -a -um — sure, certain
cesso -are -avi cessatum — I cease, stop
cinis cineris m. — ash
circa (preposition + acc.) — around, about, approximately
circum (preposition + acc.) — around
circus -i m. — chariot racing track
cista -ae f. — box, chest (old Eng. 'c' → 'ch' before 'e')
cito -are — I rouse, stir up (*excite* etc.)
cito adv. — quickly
civis is m/f. — citizen
clarus -a -um — bright, clear, famous
claudo (-clud) -ere clausi cl(a)usum — I shut
clemens clementis — kind, merciful
codex codicis m. — writing tablets (cf. *codicil*)
cognosco -ere cognovi cognitum — I find out, learn, know
cogo -ere — I compel
collega -ae m. — partner in office, colleague
collum -i n. — neck
colo -ere colui cultum — I till, cultivate; worship
communis -e — common, public
compleo -ere -evi completum — I fill
compono -ere -posui compositum — I put together (cf. *compound* from French *compondre*)
compos compotis — having control of, master of
concilio -are -avi conciliatum — I bring together, make friendly
concutio -ere -cussi concussum — I shake together, strike
condo -ere — I found, build, lay up, bury
confero -ferre -tuli collatum — I bring together, compare
confiteor -eri confessus sum — I admit, confess
congregor -ari congregatus sum — I gather together, congregate
conor -ari — I try
conservo -are -avi conservatum — I preserve
constituo -ere -ui constitutum — I set up, appoint, organize
contagio -ionis f. — touching

contingo -ere -tigi contactum	I touch
coquus -i m.	cook (old Saxon *kok*, old Eng. *coc*)
cor cordis n.	heart
cornu cornus n.	horn
corona -ae f.	crown (a coroner upheld rights of the crown)
corpus corporis n.	body
corrigo -ere correxi correctum	I put straight
cras adv.	tomorrow
credo -ere credidi creditum	I believe, trust, entrust
creo -are creavi creatum	I elect, appoint
cresco -ere crevi cretum	I increase
crimen criminis n.	charge, allegation
crux crucis f.	cross, critical point
culina -ae f.	kitchen (old Saxon *kukina*)
culpo -are	I blame
cum (preposition + abl.)	with
cumulus -i m.	pile, heap
cuprum -i n. (late Lat. for Cyprium)	copper (*kipper* was used by Saxons for copper coloured fish)
cura ae f.	care, attention
curo -are	I look after
curro -ere cucurri cursum	I run
custos custodis m.	guard
de (preposition + abl.)	down from: about, concerning
debeo -ere debui debitum	I owe, ought
decem	ten
decet -ere (impersonal verb)	it is seemly, becoming, fitting
decimus -a -um	tenth
declaro -are -avi declaratum	I make clear, proclaim
decorus -a -um	becoming, fitting, seemly
decus decoris n.	ornament, embellishment, honour
defendo -ere -di -sum (defensor m.)	I defend (defender)
delecto -are -avi delectatum	I delight
deleo -ere delevi deletum	I destroy, remove
delinquo -ere deliqui delictum	I do wrong
dens dentis m.	tooth
deus -i m.	god
dexter -tra -trum	right
dico -ere dixi dictum	I say, speak
dies diei m.	day
digitus -i m.	finger
diminuo -ere -ui diminutum	I lessen
dirigo -ere -exi directum	I steer, direct
disco -ere	I learn
discrimen -inis n.	distinction, difference, danger
divido ere dividi divisum	I separate, share out
do dare dedi datum	I give
doctor doctoris m.	teacher
doleo -ere	I grieve, feel pain
dominus -i m.	master, lord
drama -tis n. (borrowed from Greek)	play

dubito -are	I doubt. hesitate
duco -ere duxi ductum	I lead. guide
dulcis -e	sweet
dum	while
duo duae duo	two
duro -are -avi duratum (durus -a -um)	I make hard; endure (hard)
dux ducis m.	leader; 'duke'
e (preposition + abl.)	= ex
ebrius -a -um	drunk
edo esse edi esum	I eat
elementum -i n.	letter of alphabet, rudiment
eligo -ere elegi electum	I choose
emo -ere emi emptum (emptor m.)	I buy (buyer)
episcopus -i. m. (from Greek)	overseer, bishop
equus -i m.	horse
erro -are	I wander, make a mistake
ex (preposition + abl.)	out of, as a result of
exemplum -i n.	example
exeo -ire exii exitum	I go out (*exit*/*exeunt* = he/they go out)
exhaurio -ire -hausi exhaustum	I drink off. drain
expedio -ire -ivi expeditum	I free feet. extricate; am useful (cf. *pes*)
extra (preposition + acc.)	outside of
fabula -ae f.	tale, story (cf. *for*)
facies faciei f.	face, appearance
facio -ere feci factum	I make, do
fallo -ere fefelli falsum	I deceive
fama -ae f.	rumour, repute, fame (cf. *for*)
fasces fascium m.	bundles of rods, symbol of a consul's power
fatum -i n.	fate, destiny (what has been spoken: cf. *for*)
felicitas felicitatis f.	success, happiness
fero ferre tuli latum	I carry, bear
ferrum -i n.	iron
fibula -ae f.	pin, clasp
fides fidei f.	faith
figo -ere fixi fixum	I attach
findo -ere fidi fissum	I split
finio -ire -ivi finitum (finis -is m.)	I set bounds to, finish (limit, end)
fio fieri factus sum	I become, happen, am made
fiscus -i m.	money chest
flagro -are -avi flagratum	I burn, blaze
flamma -ae f.	flame, fever heat
flecto -ere flexi flexum	I bend
floreo -ere	I flourish
fluo -ere	I flow
foedus foederis n.	treaty, alliance (federation, federal)
foetidus -a -um	foul-smelling, stinking
folium -ii n.	leaf
for fari fatus sum	I speak
forma -ae f.	shape, appearance, beauty
formosus -a -um	beautiful

formula -ae f. — small mould. rule. method
forum -i n. (forensis -e) — market-place (public. judicial)
fossa -ae f. — ditch
fragilis -e — easily broken
frango -ere fregi fractum — I break
frater fratris m. — brother
fraus fraudis f. — deceit. fraud
frons frontis m. — forehead
fulmen fulminis n. — lightning, thunderbolt
fumus -i m. — smoke
fundo -ere fudi fusum — I pour
fungus -i. m. — mushroom, fungus
furtim adv. — furtively. like a thief
futurus -a -um — about to be. future

gemini -orum m. — twins
genu -us n. — knee
genus generis n. — kind. type. family
gero -ere gessi gestum — I wage. conduct
gladius -ii m. — sword
glans glandis f. — acorn
gradior -i (-gressus sum) — I step. go
grandis -e — great, pompous
gratia -ae f. — grace, favour, esteem. influence
gratus -a -um — pleasing. thankful
gravis -e — heavy, serious
gubernator -is m. — helmsman (also used as a political metaphor)
guberno -are — I steer: govern

habeo -ere — I have
habito -are -avi habitatum — I live. dwell
haero -ere haesi haesum (-hes) — I stick
herba ae f. — grass
heres heredis m/f. — heir
hilaris -e — cheerful
homo hominis m. — human being
honorarium -ii n. — fee
horreo -ere — I bristle, shudder at, am alarmed
horror horroris m. — bristling, dread, horror
hortus -i m. — garden
hospes hospitis m/f. — host, friend
humilis -e — humble

iaceo -ere — I lie, am situated
iacio -ere ieci iactum (-iectum) — I throw
ibidem adv. — in the same place
id est — that is
idem (abbrev. id) eadem idem — the same
ignis -is m. — fire
ignoro -are — I do not know
immineo -ere — I lean towards, hang over
imperium -ii n. — power, empire, command
implico -are -avi implicatum — I infold, envelop

imprimo -ere -pressi impressum — I press on. print
impune adv. — with impunity
in (preposition + acc. & abl.) — in, on, into, on to
index indicis m/f. — informer, sign, catalogue
inferior inferioris — lower
inficio -ere -feci infectum — I dip in, dye, stain, taint
inicio -ere -ieci iniectum — I throw in
initium -ii n. (initio -are) — beginning (I begin, originate)
iniuria -ae f. — something done contrary to justice, wrong
insula -ae f. — island
integer integra integrum — untouched, whole
inter (preposition + acc.) — between, among
interest — it matters, makes a difference
interim adv. — meanwhile
invenio -ire inveni inventum — I come upon, find, discover
ipse ipsa ipsum — -self
iterum adv. (itero -are) — again (I repeat)
iudex iudicis m. (iudico -are) — judge (I judge)
iudicium -ii n. — court, trial, judgement
iugum -i n. — yoke
iungo -ere iunxi iunctum — I join
iuro -are (periuria -ae f.) — I swear (false swearing, perjury)
ius iuris n. — right, law
iustus -a -um — right, fair, just
iuxta (preposition + acc.) — near, close to

labor labi lapsus sum — I slip
laboro -are -avi laboratum — I work
lacesso -ere -ivi lacessitum — I provoke
laedo -ere laesi laesum (les) — I hurt, harm
lapsus -us m. — slip (cf. *labor*)
largus -a -um — abundant, plentiful
larva -ae f. — ghost, skeleton
lateo -ere — I am hidden
latus -a -um — wide, broad
latus lateris n. — side
laudo -are -avi laudatum — I praise
lego -are — I bequeath
lego -ere legi lectum (lector -is m.) — I read (reader)
lenio -ire (lenis -e) — I soften, soothe (soft, gentle)
lente adv. — slowly
leo leonis m. — lion
levo -are (levis -e) — I lift (light)
lex legis f. — law
liber -era -erum (liberalis -e) — free (befitting a free man, generous)
libero -are -avi liberatum — I set free
libertas libertatis f. — freedom
libet -ere libuit libitum — it pleases
libra -ae f. — pound; plural = balance, scales
licet impersoal verb (licitus -a -um) — it is allowed (lawful, legitimate)
lignum -i n. — firewood, timber
ligo -are -avi ligatum — I bind

limes limitis m. (limito -are)	boundary (I enclose within bounds)
lingua -ae f.	tongue
liquidus -a -um	flowing
loco -are -avi locatum	I place
locus -i m.	place
longus -a -um	long
loquor loqui locutus sum	I speak
lubricus -a -um	slippery
lucerna -ae f.	lamp. light
lucidus -a -um (lux lucis f.)	bright. clear, full of light (light)
ludo -ere lusi lusum	I play
lumen luminis n.	light. lamp
macula -ae f.	spot, stain
magnus -a -um	big. large. great
maiestas maiestatis f.	greatness. majesty
maior maius	greater
male adv.	badly
mando -are -avi mandatum	I entrust. instruct
maneo -ere mansi mansum	I remain. stay
manus -us f.	hand
mare maris n.	sea
marinus -a -um	of the sea
massa -ae f.	lump. mass
medicus -i m.	doctor
medius -a -um	middle
mel mellis n.	honey
melior melioris	better
memoro -are	I recall
mens mentis f.	mind
mensis mensis m.	month
mergo -ere mersi mersum	I drown. overwhelm
metallum -i n.	mine
metior -iri mensus sum	I measure
migro -are -avi migratum	I move, depart
miles militis m. (milito -are)	soldier (I do military service. wage war)
mille	a thousand
minister ministri m. (ministro -are)	servant (I serve, manage, govern)
minor minus	lesser, smaller
miror -ari miratus sum	I am surprised, wonder at
mitigo -are -avi mitigatum (mitis -e)	I make mild, assuage, pacify (mild, gentle)
mitto -ere misi missum	I send
modus -i m.	manner. way, means
mollis -e (mollio -ire)	soft (I soften, moderate)
monachus -i m (medieval Latin)	monk
moneo -ere monui monitum	I advise, warn, admonish
mons montis m.	mountain, hill
monumentum -i n.	memorial
morior mori mortuus sum	I die
mors mortis f.	death
moveo -ere movi motum	I move
multus -a -um	much, many

municipium -ii n.	self-governing town
munus -eris n. (munificentia -ae f.)	service (generosity. liberality. munificence)
mus muris m.	mouse
mutabilis -e	fickle, changeable
muto -are -avi mutatum	I change
nascor nasci natus sum	I am born
nasus -i m.	nose
natalis -e	of birth (adj.) (e.g. dies natalis = birthday)
natio nationis f.	tribe, people
nausea -ae f.	sea-sickness
navigo -are -avi navigatum	I sail
navis -is f.	ship
neco -are	I kill
neglego -ere neglexi neglectum	I ignore, neglect
negotium -ii n. (neotior -ari)	business (I do business)
nemo neminis m.	no one
nepos nepotis m.	grandson, relative
niger nigra nigrum	black
nihil (and nil)	nothing
nisi	unless
niteo -ere	I shine, glitter
nobilis -e	well known, famous, high-born
noceo -ere	I hurt, harm
noli!	don't!
nomen nominis n.	name
nomino -are -avi nominatum	I name
non	not
nonus -a -um	ninth
noto -are	I note
novem	nine
novus -a -um	new
nox noctis f.	night
numerus -i m.	number
numero -are -avi numeratum	I count, enumerate
nuntio -are	I announce
obeo -ire obii obitum	I die (obiit = he died)
occasio occasionis f.	opportunity, appropriate time
occupo -are -avi occupatum	I take possession of
octavus -a -um (octo)	eighth (eight)
oculus -i m.	eye
odor odoris m.	smell, scent, fragrance
officium -ii n.	duty
omen ominis n.	omen
omnis -e (omnes/omnia)	every, all (all people/things)
onus oneris n.	burden, load
operor -ari -atus	I work on
opto -are	I choose
origo originis f.	origin, beginning
oro -are -avi oratum (orator m.)	I beg (pleader, speaker)
os oris n.	mouth
ovis -is f.	sheep

paene adv. (pen-)	almost
panis panis m.	bread
par paris	equal
parens parentis m/f.	parent
paro -are -avi paratum	I prepare
pars partis f. (partes — plural)	part (a party. faction)
parvus -a -um	small. little
passim adv.	everywhere
patina -ae f.	broad shallow dish. pan
patior -i passus sum	I suffer
patria -ae f.	fatherland. country
patricius -a -um	ancestral. noble
pax pacis f.	peace
pecco -are	I sin. do wrong
pectus pectoris n.	chest
pecunia -ae f.	money
pello -ere pepuli pulsum	I drive
pelvis -is f.	basin
pendeo -ere pependi	I hang (down). am suspended
pendo -ere pependi pensum	I weigh out. pay
per (preposition + acc.)	through. along. during. in the course of
peregrinus -a -um	of a stranger or foreigner (adj.)
persona -ae f.	mask. character. person
perturbo -are -avi perturbatum	I disturb. throw into confusion
pes pedis m.	foot
peto -ere petivi petitum	I seek. aim at
pila -ae f. (dimin. pilula)	ball
piper piperis n.	pepper
pirum -i n.	pear
piscis -is m.	fish
pisum -i n.	leguminous plant. pease. pea
pius -a -um	dutiful. pious
placeo -ere	I please
placo -are -avi placatum	I appease. placate. calm
plaudo -ere plausi plausum (plod/s)	I clap
plico -are plicavi plicatum	I fold. double up (cf. *pliant*)
plebs plebis f. (plebeius -a -um)	common people (of the commons. plebeian)
ploro -are	I cry out, weep. lament
plumbum -i n.	lead
plus pluris	more
poena -ae f.	penalty
pompa -ae f.	solemn procession
pondo adv.	in weight (pound, after *libra* was omitted)
pondus ponderis n.	weight (cf. *pendo*)
pono -ere posui positum	I place, put
populus -i m.	people, nation
porcus -i m.	pig
porto -are	I carry
possum posse	I am able
post (preposition + acc.)	after
potens potentis	powerful
potio potionis f.	drink, draught

praecipito -are -avi -atum (cf. *caput*)   I send headlong (cf. *precipice*)
prehendo -ere -di prehensum   I grasp. take
primus -a -um   first
principalis -e   first, original, chief
pro (preposition + abl.)   for, before, on behalf of. in proportion to
proles -is f. (proletarius -a -um)   off-spring (producing children — see p.46)
proximus -a -um   next
pudet -ere impers. vb.(repudio -are)   it shames (I put away, reject)
puer -i m.   boy
pugno -are (pugnax pugnacis)   I fight (pugnacious)
pulmo pulmonis m.   lung
puls pultis f.   thick pottage
pungo -ere punxi punctum   I pierce, prick
puto -are   I think
putridus -a -um   rotten

quadri-   fourfold
quaero -ere quaesivi quaesitum   I seek. ask. inquire
quantus -a -um   how much
quartus -a -um   fourth
quattuor   four
qui quae quod (relative pronoun)   who. which
quid (pronoun)   what. anything, something
quietus -a -um   quiet, peaceful
quinque   five
quintus -a -um   fifth
quis?   who?
quondam adv.   once, formerly
quorum (genitive plural of qui)   of whom

radius -ii m.   ray
radix radicis m.   root
ramus -i m.   branch
rapidus -a -um (rapio -ere)   tearing along, swift (I snatch)
rectus -a -um   straight
refero referre rettuli relatum   I take back, refer to
regalis -e (regalia -ium n.pl.)   belonging to a king (cf. *rex*) (royal emblems)
regina -ae f.   queen
regio -ionis f.   region, district
rego -ere rexi rectum   I rule
remedium -ii n.   cure
res rei f.   thing
resisto -ere restiti   I stand back, remain, withstand, resist
respondeo -ere -di responsum   I reply, answer
respublica reipublicae f.   republic, state
rex regis m. (adj. regalis -e)   king (royal)
rideo -ere risi risum   I laugh, smile
rigor rigoris m.   stiffness
robur roboris n.   strength
robustus -a -um   strong
rodo -ere rosi rosum   I gnaw
ros roris n.   dew

rostrum -i n.	beak. prow: platform
rumpo -ere rupi ruptum	I break
rus ruris n.	the countryside
saccus -i m.	bag, sack
sacer sacra sacrum	sacred
sacerdos sacerdotis m/f.	priest
sagitta -ae f. (sagittarius -i m.)	arrow (archer)
sanctus -a -um	holy (a saint)
sanguis sanguinis m.	blood
sano -are (late Lat. sanatorius -a -um)	I heal (giving health)
sanus -a -um	healthy, sound
satelles satellitis m.	attendant
satis adv.	enough
scando -ere	I climb (see also *ascendo*)
sceleratus -a -um (scelus -eris n.)	wicked (crime)
scientia -ae f.	knowledge
scorpio -ionis m.	scorpion
scribo -ere scripsi scriptum	I write. draw
seco -are secui sectum	I cut
secretus -a -um	set apart. secret (→ secretary via Italian)
secundus -a -um	following. second
securus -a -um	free from care
sedeo -ere sedi sessum	I sit (sedimentum = settlement)
sella -ae f.	seat. chair
semen seminis n.	seed
semper adv.	always
sententia -ae f.	opinion
sentio -ire sensi sensum	I feel
septem	seven
septimus -a -um	seventh
septuaginta	seventy
sequor -i secutus sum	I follow
sex	six
sextus -a -um	sixth
siccus -a -um	dry
sido -ere	I sit, settle
silva -ae f.	wood (cf. Sylvia, Sylvester)
sine (preposition + abl.)	without
singuli -ae -a (simplex)	one at a time (once folded, simple)
sisto -ere	I cause to stand; I stand
socius ii m. (socialis -e)	ally, (belonging to allies)
societas societatis f.	alliance, community
sol solis m.	sun
sollicito -are	I stir, agitate, instigate
solvo -ere solvi solutum	I undo, release, pay
somnus -i m.	sleep
sono -are	I sound
sonus -i m.	sound
spargo -ere sparsi sparsum	I scatter, sprinkle
species speciei f.	appearance, form
speciosus -a -um	attractive, good-looking, showy
spero -are	I hope

spicio -ere spexi spectum — I look
spina -ae f. — thorn
spiro -are -avi spiratum (spiritus -us) — I breathe (breath, spirit)
status -us m. (cf. sto) — position
stella -ae f. — star
sterno -ere stravi stratum — I stretch out, spread, throw down
sterilis -e — barren
stimulus -i m. — goad, spur, incentive
stipendium -ii n. — pay
sto -are steti statum — I stand
studeo -ere — I am eager, support
stupeo -ere — I am stunned with amazement
suadeo -ere suasi suasum — I urge
sub (preposition + abl.) — under
substantia -ae f. — (standing underneath), being, matter
suffragium -ii n. — vote
suggero -ere (late Lat. suggestio f.) — I carry under, supply, advise (a suggestion)
sui (genitive of pronoun se) — of oneself
summus -a -um (summa -ae f.) — highest, greatest (chief point, height, sum)
super (preposition + acc.) — over, on
supercilium -ii n. — eyebrow
superior superioris — higher, upper
supero -are — I overcome, conquer
supremus -a -um — highest, final, ultimate
surgo -ere surrexi surrectum — I rise, get up
suspendo -ere -di suspensum — I hang under
sylv- — see *silva*

tango -ere tetigi tactum — I touch
taurus -i m. — bull
tegulae -arum f. — roof covering, tiles
tellus telluris f. — earth
tempus temporis n. — time
tendo -ere tetendi tentum/tensum — I stretch
teneo -ere tenui tentum — I hold
terminus -i m. — limit, boundary
terra -ae f. — land, earth
terreo -ere — I frighten
tertius -a -um — third
testis -is m/f. (testimonium -ii n.) — witness (evidence)
testor -ari (testamentum -i n.) — I give evidence, make a will (a will)
tolero -are -avi toleratum — I bear, endure, sustain
torqueo -ere torsi tortum — I twist, turn
tot — so many (*tot...quot* = as many as)
totus tota totum — whole
tracto -are — I handle, manage
trado -ere tradidi traditum — I hand over, pass on
traho -ere traxi tractum — I pull, drag
tres tria — three
triumpus -i m. (triumpho -are) — victory procession (I celebrate a triumph)
tutamen tutaminis n. — protection

ultra (preposition + acc.)	beyond, more than
uncia -ae f.	a twelfth part (hence *inch* and *ounce*)
universi -ae -a	all together
unus una unum	one
urbs urbis f.	city
ursa ae f.	bear
uva -ae f.	grape
uxor -is f.	wife
vacca -ae f.	cow
vaco -are -avi vacatum	I am empty, at leisure
vado -ere (-vasi -vasum)	I go
vagor -ari	I wander, roam
valeo -ere (valent -: cf. Valentine)	I am strong, of value, fare well
validus -a -um	strong
vallum -i n.	rampart
varius -a -um	different, various, varied
Vectis -is f.	Isle of Wight
vehor vehi vectus sum	I travel, am carried, ride
vena -ae f.	vein
venio -ire veni ventum	I come
venter ventri m.	stomach
ventus -i m.	wind
verbum -i n.	word
veritas veritatis f.	truth
verna -ae m/f. (vernaculus -a -um)	home-bred slave (native, indigenous)
versor -ari versatus sum	I am engaged in
vertebra -ae f.	joint, vertebra
verto -ere verti versum	I turn
verus -a -um	true
via -ae f.	road
vice	in turn, instead of
vicinus -a -um	neighbouring
videlicet	(you may see), evidently, namely
video -ere vidi visum	I see
vigilo -are	I am awake, watchful, vigilant
vinco -ere vici victum	I conquer
vinum -i n.	wine
violentus -a -um	viloent
violo -are -avi violatum	I treat with violence, injure
virgo -inis f.	girl, maiden
vita -ae f.	life
vitis -is f.	vine
vito -are (also *evito*)	I avoid
vivo -ere vixi victum (vivus -a -um)	I live (alive, living)
voco -are -avi vocatum	I call
volo velle volui (volent)	I wish
volvo -ere volvi volutum	I roll
voro -are (vorax voracis)	I swallow whole, devour (devouring)
vox vocis f.	voice
vulnero -are (vulnus vulneris n.)	I wound (a wound)